ENDORSE

God wants to use you as a vessel to demonstrate His love, goodness, and power to those around you! In Tracy Cooke's book, *Heavenly Secrets to Unwrapping Your Spiritual Gifts*, your heart will be awakened to be God's ambassador and manifest His Kingdom wherever you go. I pray that your heart is encouraged, refreshed, and deeply impacted by the truths contained in this powerful book!

> RYAN BRUSS, author of *Carrying the Presence: How to Bring Kingdom of God to Anyone, Anywhere* and *Living Loved: Awakening Your Heart to the Father's Love*

I'm endorsing this powerful book written by my spiritual son, Prophet Tracy. I encourage everyone to get this book. It truly unlocks the keys of the Holy Spirit to help you walk in the power of the supernatural and to be very powerful in your ministry to be used by God. There is a price to pay for this anointing and Tracy has paid it.

Tracy has been stamped in the image of our Lord, and he is being spent for His glory. Great revival is coming and this book will get you ready. God bless you and thank you very much for your prayers and all the time you spent seeking God for these great revelations to share with the Body of Christ.

> PROPHET GLENDA JACKSON

Heavenly Secrets

TO UNWRAPPING YOUR

Spiritual GIFTS

Heavenly Secrets

TO UNWRAPPING YOUR

Spiritual GIFTS

Start Moving
in the Gifts of the
Holy Spirit Today!

TRACY COOKE

It's Supernatural! and Messianic Vision Inc.

Cover design by Eileen Rockwell

Interior design by Terry Clifton

For more information on foreign distributors, call 717-532-3040.

Reach us on the Internet: www.destinyimage.com.

ISBN 13 TP: 978-0-7684-5718-6

ISBN 13 eBook: 978-0-7684-5719-3

ISBN 13 HC: 978-0-7684-5721-6

ISBN 13 LP: 978-0-7684-5720-9

For Worldwide Distribution, Printed in the U.S.A.

1 2 3 4 5 6 7 8 / 24 23 22 21 20

CONTENTS

FOREWORD

I have had the privilege of meeting and becoming friends of many great men and women of God, especially those that operate in the Holy Spirit and His gifts. As a new believer, I met and developed a friendship with Kathryn Kuhlman. She interviewed me twice on her national television show. She even offered to mentor me as we met when I was a few months old in the Lord. One of my regrets is I did not realize at the time how special she was and I declined the mentoring. After all, what she did was just normal. Normal as defined by the Bible. Little did I know, she had the strongest anointing of her generation and perhaps the strongest since Jesus walked in the flesh! Perhaps this is why I look for those that walk deeply in the Holy Spirit. I pride myself in finding unknowns and giving them a platform to teach and demonstrate their gifts from God to the world.

Shortly, over a billion, mostly young people, will be radically saved. The old wineskins of most churches will not satisfy them. They will be radically saved and baptized in the Holy Spirit and FIRE! The next and greatest move of God's Spirit in history is upon us. It is called the Greater Glory. It will be 100 times more powerful than Kathryn Kuhlman or any great ministry the world has ever seen. The Greater Glory is like the water that came from Ezekiel's Temple. First it was at ankle level and gradually the water increased until it was a river. And everywhere it went, fish or people were healed. Right now the glory is at your ankles. Get hungry for more. It is about to become a mighty river. My heart's desire is for you to be front and center in this Greater Glory outpouring. God is saying, "all hands on deck!" Now is the time to prepare.

One such unknown I have interviewed and will be a great teacher for you is my friend Tracy Cooke. I first met Tracy Cooke in an airport. Then many years later a frequent guest, prophetess, Glenda Jackson said God told her I should interview him. At the same time my main intercessor had to stop praying for me for personal reasons. He had prayed for me for years and I felt the loss. I have always had one main intercessor that prays many hours every day for me, especially for my Jewish evangelistic meetings. But at the exact same time the first intercessor left, God told Tracy to start praying for me. God is so good!

This is what I know first hand about Tracy. He prays in tongues almost all night. Every night. He is a humble man that walks in the reverential fear of the Lord. He has the keenest and most specific word of knowledge ministry I have ever seen. His gift of prophecy is also extremely precise and accurate. He has great intimacy with the Holy Spirit. He carries a degree of the same anointing as William Branham. It is my belief, it will soon be at Branham's level or higher.

He teaches not from study or intellect, although he knows the Word well, but from the Spirit of God. He does not teach anything he has not walked in for many years. I believe if you apply his revelatory teaching you too will have great intimacy with the Holy Spirit and operate in all the gifts of the Holy Spirit.

This is my prayer for all that read this book.

> *"Eye has not seen,*
> *nor ear heard,*
> *nor has it entered into your heart,*
> *the things which God has prepared for*
> *you because you love Him."*
> (1 CORINTHIANS 2:9 MEV personalized)

Blessings and Global Glory,

SID ISRAEL ROTH

1 | YOUR GREAT ASSIGNMENT IN LIFE

*U*nlocking the spiritual gifts in your life requires heavenly keys. These are the keys that will help you find your gifting, uncover your calling, and understand how the Holy Spirit can work in your life in order to manifest God's purpose through you. God longs to fulfill His great commission through you, revealing His glory on the earth.

Engaging with this journey of discovering your spiritual gifts requires an intimate relationship with the Holy Spirit. Learning to follow His lead is absolutely crucial to fulfilling God's assignment for your life. My prayer would be that this first chapter would introduce a study of God's Word that leads to a deeper understanding of the Holy Spirit. I have faith that, as you read, you will begin to experience His presence, become tender to His convictions, and learn how He engages with your life and guides you to fulfill God's perfect will.

There are many misconceptions about the Holy Spirit in the 21st century Church, particularly surrounding the baptism of the Holy Spirit. Some have fallen into the misunderstanding that the baptism of fire is the same as the moment of salvation. It is not the same moment; it is one of the gifts of the Spirit. For this reason, though, I want to discuss the baptism of the Holy Spirit, and its role in the life of believers.

Many people fail to realize that the Holy Spirit is a distinct and separate member of the Holy Trinity of God. He works in association and complete harmony with the Father and the Son, yet He should not be confused with either of His divine associates. His separate role is clearly stated in First John 5:7: *"For there are three that bear record in heaven, the Father, the Word, and the Holy Spirit; and these three are one."* And, *"Go therefore and make disciples of all nations, baptizing them in the name of the Father and of the Son and of the Holy Spirit"* (Matthew 28:19).

Among some, there is a belief that receiving salvation and being born again is the same as being baptized with the Holy Spirit. I've been asked by many people, "Well, I'm saved. So, do I have the Holy Spirit?" After you have received salvation, you have the indwelling of the Holy Spirit, but you may not have the baptism of the Holy Spirit with evidence of speaking in tongues. An individual may be regenerated by the Holy Spirit—through a conversion experience—and still not be baptized with the Holy

Spirit. Regeneration by the Holy Spirit, at the moment of conversion, means there is an impartation of life. When an individual submits their life to God, confessing that He is Lord, the impartation of life from the Holy Spirit enables eternal salvation.

In the baptism of the Holy Spirit, though, there is an impartation of fire, power, and authority. The one being baptized is being equipped for the calling and service of God. This is a gift of the Holy Spirit. His baptism manifests God's desire to endow you with the power and authority necessary to your calling. John the Baptist makes this clear when he is recorded in Matthew 3:11: *"I indeed baptize you with water unto repentance, but He who is coming after me is mightier than I, whose sandals I am not worthy to carry. He will baptize you with the Holy Spirit and fire."*

We find in Scripture that, although the disciples were saved because they believed in God's Son, Jesus, they were not yet baptized in the Holy Spirit. In Luke 10:20 Jesus says, *"Nevertheless do not rejoice in this, that the spirits are subject to you, but rather rejoice because your names are written in heaven."* Jesus told them to rejoice because their souls were saved, their names were written in Heaven. But this was long before they were baptized in the Holy Spirit after waiting in the upper room. Jesus says in Luke 24:49, *"Behold, I send the Promise of My Father upon you; but tarry in the city of Jerusalem until you are endued with power from on high."* God was sending the Holy Spirit to operate in their lives, to flow on them and with them—and then for the very first time to inhabit them.

In the Old Testament, there are many examples of people operating with the anointing of the Holy Spirit. This was not just power reserved for the prophets. Some of the great examples include David, Esther, Ezra, Micah, and Abraham. The Holy Spirit would come on them and be with them to empower them during a specific time to fulfill the will of God. It wasn't until the day of Pentecost, though, that the Holy Spirit came upon people and imbued them with power from God. And now it is accessible to all believers.

God wants you to experience this phenomenon—to encounter the Holy Spirit and His gifts. Supernatural anointing is waiting for you as you step off the shoreline of unbelief and into the deep things of God. There is no need to be intimidated or succumb to the spirit of fear. Fear means false evidence appearing real. God wants you to have bold faith, having the audacity to believe and say, "I'm going after everything that God has promised me—and the Holy Spirit is a promise."

God has given you a specific assignment to fulfill on the earth, and He wants you to have the authority to release His Word onto the earth. His baptism is distinct from the moment of salvation, but it is God's will that every person receives both salvation and the empowerment of the Holy Spirit. God gave us the Holy Spirit so that we would serve the world. His desire is that, when you speak, it would be as if He was speaking. His longing is that when He walks, it would be as if you were walking in His footsteps. God invites you to walk in the shadow of His greatness, fulfilling His dream for the earth. To do this, you need the Holy Spirit.

Wait for the Power

Jesus told His disciples to wait in Jerusalem in the upper room to receive power from on high, which would fulfill His great commission. He had already been to Calvary, shed His blood, and now He was about to go back to Heaven and sit at the right hand of God the Father. Before He left, though, He told them He would send the Holy Spirit. *"'Behold, I send the Promise of My Father upon you; but tarry in the city of Jerusalem until you are endued with power from on high.' And He led them out as far as Bethany, and He lifted up His hands and blessed them. Now it came to pass, while He blessed them, that He was parted from them and carried up into heaven"* (Luke 24:49-51).

So, the disciples went to the upper room and they waited for God to send the Holy Spirit in a totally new way. In the Old Testament, the Holy Spirit would come on people without permanently dwelling in them. For example, the Bible says of Samson, *"And the Spirit of the Lord came mightily upon him, and he tore the lion apart as one would have torn apart a young goat, though he had nothing in his hand..."* (Judges 14:6). Samson was able to overcome even this ferocious opposition with the incredible strength and power given to him by the Holy Spirit.

Throughout the entire Book of Judges, when the anointing of the Holy Spirit came on Samson, he had the power to carry pillars, slay a thousand men, and shift a whole region. In one incident, he caught 300 foxes and tied their tails together. That takes a supernatural anointing of the Holy Spirit. The Holy Spirit turns ordinary people into extraordinary ones.

Likewise, when the anointing came over Mary, an ordinary woman became extraordinary. She housed the very presence of God. And that same opportunity is waiting for you today—to live with the power from on high. It was this same strength and power through the Holy Spirit that Jesus promised us when He instructed the disciples to wait after His death and resurrection. The power He spoke of is the word *dunamis,* which means "dynamite explosion." God wants you to explode. He wants you to have dynamite power, the glory of the Holy Spirit operating in your life and flowing through you for His glory.

This is the empowerment that the disciples were waiting for in that upper room. Jesus told them to wait together for the Promise of the Father, the Holy Spirit. John said of Jesus, *"He will baptize you with the Holy Spirit and fire"* (Matthew 3:11). This was the promise of the Father that, when Jesus ascended to the right hand of the heavenly Father, He would send the comfort of the Holy Spirit to operate in their lives. And because they followed His direction and waited, they were all filled with the Holy Spirit.

> *When the Day of Pentecost had fully come, they were all with one accord in one place. And suddenly there came a sound from heaven, as of a rushing mighty wind, and it filled the whole house where they were sitting. Then there appeared to them divided tongues, as of fire, and one sat upon each of them. And they were all filled with the Holy Spirit and began to speak with other tongues, as the Spirit gave them utterance* (Acts 2:1-4).

Like the disciples, when you have an encounter with the Holy Spirit, receiving His baptism and being filled with his explosive, *dunamis* power, something about your life lights up like a firework. Suddenly, you will be able to be a light in the midst of a dark world, because God's light is within you. It doesn't matter who you are, you have a mandate. You have a purpose on this earth. You have a calling that God wants you to enter into. But you need the help of the third person of the Trinity to fulfill that great calling.

As an individual created by God, no matter your status in life, you can operate in the gifts of the Spirit. You can see God forever change your life through great transformation. You can go from glory to glory, from faith to faith, and fulfill what you feel that conviction is that God has assigned you to fulfill. No one can be fully effective in ministry or in any other endeavor for God's glory, without the baptism of the Holy Spirit. His gift is not predicated upon having a particular anointing, though. The baptism is for everyone.

Thank God for His greatest gift: salvation! But, once you've received that precious gift, seek the baptism of the Holy Spirit. Only then can you receive power from on high to advance God's Kingdom until all the earth as it is in Heaven. Jesus told His disciples—and us—that the Holy Spirit would come to them and operate in their lives. Acts 1:8 also speaks of the Promise to be given: *"You shall receive power when the Holy Spirit has come upon you; and you shall be witnesses to Me both in Jerusalem, and in all Judaea and Samaria, and to the end of the earth."* We see here that the disciples were saved before they received the baptism of the Holy Spirit. They were saved, but they have not yet experienced the impartation of the Holy Spirit baptism. But Jesus promised that, when they did receive the baptism of fire, they would be powerful witnesses of Christ throughout the world.

All 120 Jewish believers who were waiting for the Promise were baptized in the upper room, so that Jesus could fulfill the great commission through them. As God, Jesus is omnipresent, omnipotent, and omnificent. As a man, Jesus was limited by His humanness in some ways. But you need to understand that He's no longer limited as a human person. He is omnipresent, He is omnipotent, and He is omniscient—moving through individuals worldwide. He's moving through you and I to fulfill His purpose on earth. When He was walking His earthly ministry, He had to depend on the same Holy Spirit, the same gifts of the Spirit; He was limited in His human form. Now, you and I carry the Holy Spirit among millions of other believers. His Gospel can be shared with people even in the most remote areas of the world. People are carrying the gifts of the Holy Spirit and the baptism of the Holy Spirit, ushering in a move of God.

SPIRITUAL AWAKENING

I believe we are living in the greatest hour of spiritual awakening. The glory of God is going to be fulfilled in this hour in greater measures than we have seen before. The Holy Spirit is getting ready to move in a greater way than He did in any of the previous revivals. It's mindboggling to think that God is going to move greater than in the days of George Whitefield, the English Evangelist. God's presence will be known near and far. The disciples understood the power and authority of having the Holy Spirit indwelling in them. These are the days in which the apostle Paul wished he was living. These are days in which Simon Peter wished he was alive.

You become unstoppable when you have the baptism of the Holy Spirit in your life. Once the disciples experienced the baptism, the Holy Spirit wasn't just occasionally on them or with them. After the day of Pentecost in the upper room, the Holy Spirit was within them. The New Living Translation of the Bible describes it this way: *"Then, what looked like flames or tongues of fire appeared and settled on each of them. And everyone present was filled with the Holy Spirit and began speaking in other languages, as the Holy Spirit gave them this ability"* (Acts 2:3-4).

The disciples and others who were in the upper room were experiencing Jesus' prophecy: "Wait until the other side of Me comes, wait until you get this power from on high, your ministry will be entirely different from My ministry. Where I was limited, you will not be limited—you will have the power of the Holy Spirit and He will give you the authority not just over devils, sin, sickness, and diseases, but the Holy Spirit will be your comfort. He will console you in the dark seasons of your life as well."

And this happened because they obeyed Jesus, and they waited. So often we don't want to wait. We don't want to be patient. We are always in a hurry. The hardest thing in the world is to wait. But let me tell you, faith is like a muscle—if you don't use it, you lose it. When you can listen to God's instructions, though, and obey Him with your actions, every step you take will become easier as you follow His leading. When you're waiting on God, He is inviting you into an opportunity to experience the fulfillment of His promise in your life.

Psalm 23 speaks of the assignment David is given when God laid him down in the quiet, green pasture beside gently moving water:

> *The Lord is my shepherd; I shall not want. He makes*
> *me to lie down in green pastures; He leads me beside*

the still waters. He restores my soul; He leads me in the paths of righteousness for His name's sake. Yea, though I walk through the valley of the shadow of death, I will fear no evil; for You are with me; Your rod and Your staff, they comfort me. You prepare a table before me in the presence of my enemies; You anoint my head with oil; my cup runs over. Surely goodness and mercy shall follow me all the days of my life; and I will dwell in the house of the Lord forever (Psalm 23:1-6)

You cannot hear God in the rushing streams of life. You have to be still to hear God's voice speaking to you. By quieting yourself, by slowing down and waiting on Him, you can seek Him directly and precisely. In this way, you can focus on God's intention, not your opinions, not your desires—but on His good and perfect will for you.

And when you learn to wait well on God, His promise from Isaiah is that strength and supernatural advantage will be your portion. *"But those who wait on the Lord shall renew their strength; they shall mount up with wings like eagles, they shall run and not be weary, they shall walk and not faint"* (Isaiah 40:31). This God-given strength infuses you with the endurance to stand against any attack from the enemy. Don't be surprised if, once you receive the baptism of the Holy Spirit and you understand the new power in your life, you begin to experience some resistance. But don't be discouraged. The Holy Spirit always has the upper hand. The powers of darkness cannot overcome the power of the Holy Spirit and His gifts in our lives.

AVAILABLE TO EVERYONE

At the day of Pentecost, experiencing the power of the Holy Spirit on the disciples, thousands of people came to Christ. God was moving powerfully, but the enemy was also doing his best to stop it. Saul of Tarsus became the great apostle Paul, but prior to his conversion and subsequent baptism of the Holy Spirit, he was doing everything he could to stop Christians. Portions of Acts 9:1-17 read as following:

> *Then Saul, still breathing threats and murder against the disciples of the Lord, went to the high priest and asked letters from him to the synagogues of Damascus, so that if he found any who were **of the Way**, whether men or women, he might bring them bound to Jerusalem.*
>
> *As he journeyed he came near Damascus, and suddenly a light shone around him from heaven. Then he fell to the ground, and heard a voice saying to him, "Saul, Saul, why are you persecuting Me?" And he said, "Who are You, Lord?" Then the Lord said, "I am Jesus, whom you are persecuting.*
>
> *...Then Saul arose from the ground, and when his eyes were opened he saw no one. But they led him by the hand and brought him into Damascus. And he was three days without sight, and neither ate nor drank.*
>
> *Now there was a certain disciple at Damascus named Ananias; and to him the Lord said in a vision,*

"Ananias." And he said, "Here I am, Lord." So the Lord said to him, "Arise and go to the street called Straight, and inquire at the house of Judas for one called Saul of Tarsus...."

*Then Ananias answered, "Lord, I have heard from many about this man, how much harm he has done to Your saints in Jerusalem. And here he has authority from the chief priests to bind all who call on Your name." But the Lord said to him, "Go, for he is a chosen vessel of Mine...." And Ananias went his way and entered the house; and laying his hands on him he said, "Brother Saul, **the Lord Jesus, who appeared to you on the road as you came, has sent me** that you may receive your sight and **be filled with the Holy Spirit**."*

I encourage you to read the entire passage. It is filled with Paul's experience on the road to Damascus. His miraculous testimony illuminates how God can change and use an individual no matter who they are, what their background is, or what their pedigree in life is. You may not have been born with a silver spoon in your mouth, you may not feel qualified, you may not feel educated—but when the Holy Spirit comes upon you, you become extraordinary and before you know it, you're speaking in the language of Heaven. Like Peter standing up to preach on the day of Pentecost, you will speak with such authority that God will use you to touch the people around you with His power, truth, and love.

On the road to Damascus, the apostle Paul experienced a miraculous conversion as the voice of the Lord spoke to him. Saul was on his way to stop the move of God, but God intervened supernaturally. It would have been terrifying for Ananias to obey God's instructions to visit Saul, a known killer of Christians. But, being filled with the Holy Spirit, he obeyed. And, because of his obedience, Saul's very identity was transformed.

The Holy Spirit residing within us, from His baptism, is that which empowers us to pray for our enemies and those who do us harm. Many times, we're so quick to judge and condemn people. But, as Paul's transformation highlights, we never know how God is planning on using individuals for His Kingdom. Even those who seem to oppose us, to work against God's plan, are His beloved children. We need the baptism of the Holy Spirit so that we can see them with His eyes and operate in the love of God.

OPPOSITION CULTIVATES GLORY

The Holy Spirit is the one who helps us to see a person for their spirit instead of judging them as a demonic force who is attempting to stop our lives or ministry. A person might be bound by the demonic, but that is not their identity. And God always has the final word. Truthfully, nothing brings the glory of God on your life like opposition. So, when you see someone trying to work against you and you feel the enemy is setting plots against you, you actually may be very close to an extraordinary God encounter.

This is exactly what happened to Saul on the road to Damascus. He was ready with signed documents authorizing him to stop those followers of Jesus. He had gone to the high priest and asked for letters from him to take to the synagogues in Damascus, stating that if he found anyone who was "of the way," he could imprison or even kill them. The terminology "of the way" meant the followers of Christ. This is before they were called Christians. Jesus says in John 14:6, *"I am the way, the truth, and the life."*

Saul of Tarsus had an agenda: to find and punish believers in Jesus. As he journeyed toward Damascus, suddenly a light shone around him from Heaven. He fell to the ground and heard a voice say to him, "Saul, Saul, why are you prosecuting me?" He said, "Who are you, Lord? Then the Lord said, "I am Jesus, whom you are prosecuting." Saul, trembling and astonished, said, "Lord, what do You want me to do?" So here is Saul who had a plan and agenda to stop the move of God—but God stopped Saul and told him His plan and agenda, instead. Saul would no longer stop Christians from spreading the good news that Jesus was alive. He had an encounter with the Holy Spirit, with Jesus, and his life changed completely. Everything he thought he knew was wrong, and he realized he couldn't stop what God had ordained. Soon enough Saul would be Paul—a man who would be instrumental in spreading the good news himself.

The obedient Christians who sat in the upper room received authority from the Holy Spirit who sits on the right hand of the heavenly Father. From that infilling of the Holy Spirit, they began to share the Gospel of Jesus with signs and wonders and miracles. And, because of this ordained move of God, Saul of Tarsus found himself in the vulnerable position of being convicted on the road to Damascus. The Lord asked him why he was trying to stop what

He ordained. And Saul asks, "Lord, who are You?" With that question, Saul was set up to receive salvation.

Saul was highly educated, trained by Gamaliel in the ways of religion. He was one of the finest of students and very knowledgeable about Jewish law. Yet he didn't know the truth about Jesus or the Holy Spirit until he was knocked off of his mule and fell to the ground on his face. The Lord said, *"Arise and go into the city and you will be told what you must do"* (Acts 9:6). God gave Saul instructions, and he obeyed. When you walk with the Lord, He is faithful to give instructions for what you need to do when advancing your walk with the Lord. There are always instructions.

Once he received direction from the Lord, Saul got off of the ground and realized that he was blind. The men traveling with him stood speechless having heard a voice, but not having seen anyone. Humbled in mind, body, and spirit, Saul was led by the hand into Damascus. For three days and three nights, he lay in the house of Judas without eating or drinking.

But the Lord wasn't done with him. God came to Ananias in a vision, giving him the spiritual gift of a word of knowledge. The Lord gave Ananias the name of the street where he would find Saul. As he's receiving this word of knowledge, though, Ananias felt scared. He knew that Saul was a dangerous man to anyone following Christ. Even though the gift of the word of knowledge was operating in his life, fear came over him. In essence he said, "Wait a second Lord, I've heard from many about this man, how much harm he has done to Your saints in Jerusalem. And he has authority from the chief priests to bind all who call on Your name."

Now think about it, Saul was given authority from the chief priests to stop a move of God. Religion will always try to stop advancement in your relationship with God. Religion will harm you, but your relationship with God will build you up. Dear reader, you don't need religion, you need a relationship with the Almighty God. And when you get on fire for God, religion will have to step back and give room for a relationship with God.

Although Ananias operated in the gift of the word of knowledge from God, he was intimidated by Saul's history. *The key to remember here is that fear becomes a weapon of mass destruction to your spiritual life.* When you operate in fear, the damage can be devastating. But if you continue in the grace of the Lord Jesus Christ and the faith of the Holy Spirit, you can dominate fear. Always remember, *"God has not given us a spirit of fear, but of power and of love and of a sound mind"* (2 Timothy 1:7).

Ananias argued with the Lord because of fear. But he chose to obey God's voice, instead of his fear, and he went to Saul. The Lord said that He wanted Ananias to lay hands on Saul because He gave him authority above the spirit of fear. Don't worry about what "they" say, worry about what God is saying to you. If you can get past the fear of people, you can get to God.

The Lord said to Ananias, *"Go, for he is a chosen vessel of Mine to bear My name...."* This declaration reminds me of the verse, *"For many are called, but few are chosen"* (Matthew 22:14, see also Matthew 20:16).

When you're chosen by God to be a vessel or instrument to bear His name, wherever God assigns you to, whatever position He puts you in, realize that when you are chosen, you have all of

Heaven backing you up. God will break the spirit of intimidation and fear. He will raise you out of low self-esteem. He will square your shoulders with confidence and straighten your paths for forward movement. In other words, He ordained your steps to where He wants to lead you. The Bible says He guides us, He directs us, and He leads us by His Holy Spirit every day of our lives if we call upon Him.

The name Ananias means a gift of consolation. God sent His gift of consolation to Saul in his moment of weakness and repentance. Likewise, you too can be a consolation to other. You can console people in their time of sorrow. You can present joy to them when everything in their life may seem to be falling apart. You will be amazed when you receive the baptism of the Holy Spirit and realize how you can fit into other people's lives around you.

So, Ananias, operating in the gift of word of knowledge, follows God's instructions to go to a direct place of destiny. The Lord tells Ananias that Saul of Tarsus has been born again, but that he needs to hear the Good News. And God wants Ananias to lay hands on Saul so he can receive the baptism of the Holy Spirit.

> *And Ananias went his way and entered the house; and laying his hands on him he said, "Brother Saul, the Lord Jesus, who appeared to you on the road as you came, has sent me that you may receive your sight and be filled with the Holy Spirit." Immediately there fell from his eyes something like scales, and he received his sight at once; and he arose and was baptized* (Acts 9:17-18).

The glory of God was so powerful, the encounter so incredible, that Saul became the great apostle Paul, writing much of the New Testament. Since his encounter, he has millions of people's lives over the centuries. When you get into the glory realm and the Holy Spirit comes on you, like He did to Paul, you can tap into God's Kingdom and release it on the earth. From spiritual blindness to spiritual clarity—this is a realm of glory we can all experience.

Prayer of Impartation

Father, in the name of Jesus, to all that desire to have the understanding and the wanting to pursue the greatest part of life, I pray that they will discover within this chapter the keys to unlocking the heavenly gift of the Holy Spirit. Each day my prayer is first and foremost, that they have an understanding of the meaning of life in Christ and the fullness thereof. So, Lord I pray that you reveal who you are in everyone's life as they draw closer to the Holy Spirit. In Jesus' name, amen.

The thief cometh not, but for to steal, and to kill, and to destroy: I am come that they might have life, and that they might have it more abundantly (John 10:10 KJV).

2 | BEYOND SALVATION

*A*ll of us will experience good times and bad times, both mountaintop and valley experiences. God has promised, though, that He will be with us through it all: *"I will never leave you nor forsake you"* (Hebrews 13:4). While Saul was undergoing his astounding transformation, God revealed to Ananias that He was going to tell Saul up front about the valleys he would experience while living for Christ. Even being chosen by God didn't mean that Saul would escape difficult times. God told Ananias, *"For I will show him* [Saul] *how many things he must suffer for My name's sake"* (Acts 9:15).

Knowing this, Ananias boldly entered the house where Saul was staying, telling him that the Lord Jesus had sent him; so

Saul could receive his sight and be filled with the Holy Spirit. *"Immediately there fell from his eyes something like scales, and he received his sight at once."* Saul, whose transformation would be later solidified by a name change to Paul, didn't waste a minute before entering into his new life. He was baptized, he ate and regained his strength, and he began to learn from the other disciples of Jesus in Damascus.

Knowing that he needed to grow as a disciple of Jesus, Paul gleaned from them everything he could so that he would be equipped to go out and spread the good news of Jesus. This is the kind of humility we can emulate. Even though we may have some knowledge, we still need to learn from those who are more mature in God's Word. With each and every step of our journey to know our heavenly Father and advance His Kingdom, He will develop our character as we become more and more like Christ.

After Paul spent time listening and learning, he set to work. *"Immediately he preached Christ in the synagogues, that He is the Son of God"* (Acts 9:20). Almost straightaway, Paul faced his first valley as a follower of Jesus: The religious leaders, having heard about his conversion, plotted to kill him. But Paul persisted, speaking boldly in the name of the Lord Jesus to the churches throughout Judea, Galilee, and Samaria: *"And walking in the fear of the Lord and in the comfort of the Holy Spirit, they were multiplied"* (Acts 9:31).

DID YOU RECEIVE THE HOLY SPIRIT?

As Paul traveled, preaching the Gospel, he met some fellow believers who were disciples. However, when Paul asked them if they had received the Holy Spirit when they saved, they said they didn't know what he was talking about.

> *And it happened, while Apollos was at Corinth, that* **Paul,** *having passed through the upper regions, came to Ephesus. And finding some disciples he* **said to them, "Did you receive the Holy Spirit when you believed?"** *So they said to him, "We have not so much as heard whether there is a Holy Spirit." And he said to them, "Into what then were you baptized?" So they said, "Into John's baptism." Then Paul said, "John indeed baptized with a baptism of repentance, saying to the people that they should believe on Him who would come after him, that is, on Christ Jesus." When they heard this,* **they were baptized in the name of the Lord Jesus. And when Paul had laid hands on them, the Holy Spirit came upon them, and they spoke with tongues and prophesied.** *Now the men were about twelve in all* (Acts 19:1-7).

Notice this: they were saved, but not yet baptized in the Holy Spirit. Then, Paul came along and shared with them about the Holy Spirit encounter he had received through the laying on of hands by Ananias. Although they were active believers, they were not baptized in the Holy Spirit until Paul laid his hands upon them. These men in Ephesus were saved, believers of the Gospel, and referred to as disciples by the Scripture. The word "disciple" means student, one with a ready mind, one who is taught. In other words, a student has a teachable spirit. When they heard that they were missing a part of the Gospel message, they immediately wanted the baptism of the Holy Spirit. And, immediately they were filled with the Spirit and operating in the spiritual gifts.

BOUNDARIES FOR HOLY SPIRIT BAPTISM

Before Paul's conversion, Philip was preaching Christ in Samaria:

> *Then Philip went down to the city of Samaria and preached Christ to them. And the multitudes with one accord heeded the things spoken by Philip, hearing and seeing the miracles which he did. For unclean spirits, crying with a loud voice, came out of many who were possessed; and many who were paralyzed and lame were healed. And there was great joy in that city* (Acts 8:5-8).

As a result of Philip's preaching, the people accepted the Gospel and were converted; however, they were not baptized in the Holy Spirit until Peter and John came to them. These two apostles were sent from the Jerusalem church, as they heard about this move of God that was taking place in Samaria. Philip was preaching, but he did not have the gift to lay hands on them, even though he was an evangelist.

> *Now when the apostles who were at Jerusalem heard that Samaria had received the word of God, they sent* **Peter and John** *to them, who, when they had come down,* **prayed for them that they might receive the Holy Spirit**. *For as yet He had fallen upon none of them. They had only been baptized in the name of*

> the Lord Jesus. Then **they laid hands on them, and
> they received the Holy Spirit** (Acts 8:14-15).

Peter and John were reinforcements and brought with them strength and the awareness of the baptism of the Holy Spirit that they had received in the upper room. When I talk about laying on of hands, it must be understood that not everyone can lay hands on people to receive the gift of the Holy Spirit. Please understand that. That's why God selects the inner church, the fivefold ministry gifts. But if you have not received the baptism of the Holy Spirit, may I encourage you, under your church or ministry leadership, let them lay hands on you and you will receive the gift of the Holy Spirit.

> And when Simon saw that through the laying on of the apostles' hands the Holy Spirit was given, he offered them money, saying, "Give me this power also, that anyone on whom I lay hands may receive the Holy Spirit." But Peter said to him, "Your money perish with you, because you thought that the gift of God could be purchased with money! You have neither part nor portion in this matter, for your heart is not right in the sight of God" (Acts 8:18-21).

It should be clear that there are distinct differences between: 1) being saved; 2) salvation in Christ; 3) being born again; and 4) the baptism of the Holy Spirit with power and authority—they are not equal but separate experiences.

What It Isn't: Salvation

Before seeking the baptism of the Holy Spirit, you need to know what is *not*. Understanding this will help you to have a clearer understanding what it *is*. Sometimes, due to confusion, people can become frustrated while seeking the Holy Spirit and want to give up receiving His baptism. Maybe it's been one day, two days, a month, or a year without seeing any signs, so people can think, "Well, this must not be for me; it's only for other people." But this is a lie. The baptism of the Holy Spirit and speaking in tongues is available to every believer.

If you have received Jesus Christ as your Lord and Savior, you are born again. Your name is written in Lamb's Book of Life (Luke 10:20; Revelation 21:27). Being born again is not being baptized with the Holy Spirit. Let me say this very clearly—after you're saved, God wants you to go further than just being born again and attending a good church. Thank God for that! There is nothing wrong with that type of life, but salvation is just the first step. It is important to go further than salvation.

Yes, you're born again. Yes, your name is in Lamb's Book of Life, and we rejoice because that is the greatest of all miracles. But, in order for you to be effective with the message of Jesus Christ and His resurrection power, the next step is to receive the baptism of the Holy Spirit.

This is not one of the gifts that should be neglected. First Corinthians 12 talks about your prayer language. Jude 1:20-21 encourages us, *"But you, beloved, building yourselves up on your most holy faith, praying in the Holy Spirit, keep yourselves in the love of*

God…" The gift of tongues helps to build up our faith so that we can believe for the impossible. It should be clear to every believer that Christ wants you to have the power and authority of the baptism of the Holy Spirit.

What It Isn't: Water Baptism

The second thing that the baptism of the Holy Spirit is *not*—it is not being baptized in water. It is not my intention to discredit water baptism; after all, Jesus Himself was baptized in water and He is our prime example. Scripture says, *"When He had been baptized, Jesus came up immediately from the water; and behold, the heavens were opened to Him, and He saw the Spirit of God descending like a dove and alighting upon Him"* (Matthew 3:16).

Jesus also commanded His followers, and all believers, to be baptized in the name of the Father, Son, and the Holy Spirit. Water baptism consists of being dipped or immersed in water in obedience to the Lord's Word. The baptism of the Holy Spirit, on the other hand, is a supernatural encounter with the Holy Spirit. This baptism fills the individual with God's Spirit and resulting in the speaking of unknown tongues. Ephesians 5:18 (KJV) says, *"And be not drunk with wine, wherein is excess; but be filled with the Spirit."*

Many people wonder which baptism they should seek first, but the Bible shows that there is not right or wrong when it comes to the order of your baptisms. You can seek the baptism of the Holy Spirit right now while reading this book. Then you can go get baptized in water. For example, the house of Cornelius was filled with the baptism of the Holy Spirit, first, and then afterward they were baptized in water:

> While Peter was still speaking these words, **the Holy Spirit fell upon all those who heard the word.** And those of the circumcision who believed were astonished, as many as came with Peter, because the gift of the Holy Spirit had been poured out on the Gentiles also. For **they heard them speak with tongues and magnify God.** Then Peter answered, **"Can anyone forbid water, that these should not be baptized who have received the Holy Spirit just as we have?"** And **he commanded them to be baptized** in the name of the Lord. Then they asked him to stay a few days.

After the gift of the Holy Spirit came upon these people and they had spoken with tongues, Peter commanded them to be baptized in the name of the Lord and receive water baptism. Let's look back again at the Acts of the apostles: *"When they believed Philip as he preached the things concerning the kingdom of God and the name of Jesus Christ, both men and women were baptized"* (Acts 8:12). Philip the evangelist preached the things concerning the Kingdom and the name of Jesus Christ and both men and women were baptized. When Peter and John went to assist Philip, they prayed and laid their hands on the people and they received the baptism of the Holy Spirit. There was a distinct difference between the two baptisms.

WHAT IT ISN'T: SANCTIFICATION

The baptism of the Holy Spirit is also not the same as the believer's process of sanctification. The literal meaning of sanctification means preparing or setting apart a personal or thing for holy use. In Exodus 13:2, God says, *"Sanctify unto me all the firstborn, whatsoever open the womb among the children of Israel, both of man and beast, it is mine"* (KJV). Why did God want you to be sanctified? He wants you to be set apart from the world.

All of the old parts of your identity are to pass away when you come to Him, and all things are to become new. When you give your life to the Lord, you become a new creature in Him. As Paul wrote, *"Now may the God of peace Himself sanctify you completely; and may your whole spirit, soul, and body be preserved blameless at the coming of our Lord Jesus Christ"* (1 Thessalonians 5:23). So, you got let go of old ways, old behaviors, old attitudes, and adjust to the climate of sanctification by the Spirit of God in your life.

When you step into the process of sanctification, you start living a life of holiness in such a way that you feel free from the desires of sin. You don't have to strive for perfection or strive for holiness. It's not about our righteousness or holiness, but rather revealing His holiness to a world that is hungry to see what He is truly like. That's *one of the most powerful keys in walking closely with God—living a lifestyle of holiness, the best way that you can.*

That is not to say that you won't ever make a mistake or get off track. But when you do, you can return by focusing on Him and aligning with the Word of God by meditating on the

Scriptures day and night. In this way, you will have great success in all areas of life. Even when you detour away from God, taking a wrong exit because of pressure or stress, you can realign yourself with Him, saying, "Lord, here am I. I repent. Please change my heart. I want to do Your will." That's what the word "repent" means: to change not just your mind, but the condition of your heart.

When people receive and experience the sanctification by the Spirit of God, they live lives of holiness in such a way that they are freed from desires of the flesh. The Bible says the lust of the eye is the lust of the flesh and the pride of life (see 1 John 2:16). So, no one can help you kill the flesh better than the Holy Spirit. He is the one who will help you crucify the lust of the flesh, whether through fasting or His anointing. The Holy Spirit will help you subjugate sin.

Every morning I pray a prayer modeled after John the Baptist's cry, "Lord, I've got to decrease—You have to increase. I'm nothing—You are everything. Mold me, make me, shape me after Your likeness (see John 3:30). Don't let me lead myself, but You lead me by Your Holy Spirit." I encourage you to start praying that every morning and see what God does through your life as well. You'll be amazed how your life changes daily. Make a simple confession to the Holy Spirit and you will be transformed from glory to glory, from faith to faith, by the empowerment of the Holy Spirit.

First Thessalonians 4:3-8 says:

> For this is the will of God, your **sanctification**: that
> you should abstain from sexual immorality; that each

of you should know how to possess his own vessel in **sanctification** *and honor, not in passion of lust, like the Gentiles who do not know God; that no one should take advantage of and defraud his brother in this matter, because the Lord is the avenger of all such, as we also forewarned you and testified. For God did not call us to uncleanness, but in holiness. Therefore he* **who rejects this does not reject man, but God, who has also given us His Holy Spirit.**

When you are baptized with the Holy Spirit, it is not sanctification. Sanctification is the process of becoming more and more like Jesus by studying God's Word, going to church, praying to God—whatever you can do to seek more of God and turn away from wicked ways. Remember, the Word of God says, *"If My people who are called by My name will humble themselves, and pray and seek My face, and turn from their wicked ways, then I will hear from heaven, and will forgive their sin and heal their land"* (2 Chronicles 7:14).

In the Bible, God addresses clearly the kind of actions that do not please Him. But we can come to Him with humility and open our hearts up to His sanctification, praying, "Lord, this thing in my life that is displeasing to You, I want You to get rid of it. Burn it out of my life. I want to be an instrument You can flow through to touch people's lives around the world." We have the opportunity to seek the Holy Spirit for guidance, asking Him to direct every phase of our lives.

Every day we must take up our Cross and die daily to the flesh and ask God to sanctify us even more. Once you start operating in sanctification, the old desires will not resurface, the old ways, the old behaviors will fade away. You'll find that slowly but surely, you are on the Potter's wheel and He is molding you, making you like He did with the prophet, Jeremiah.

CLAY IN HIS HANDS

Jeremiah was discouraged. He was preaching and prophesying to the nation of Israel, but he thought nobody was listening. From his perspective, no one was taking heed of God's message through him. He felt so disheartened. Then the Lord said to Jeremiah:

> "Arise and go down to the potter's house, and there I will cause you to hear My words." Then I went down to the potter's house, and there he was, making something at the wheel. And the vessel that he made of clay was marred in the hand of the potter; so he made it again into another vessel, as it seemed good to the potter to make. Then the word of the Lord came to me, saying: "O house of Israel, can I not do with you as this potter?" says the Lord. "Look, as the clay is in the potter's hand, so are you in My hand, O house of Israel!"

Jeremiah wanted to give up, but the Lord told him to go to the potter's house. There, he saw the chemistry between the clay and the hands of the potter. There, he was realigned to God's perspective and resubmitted to His will.

Will you allow God to put you in His hands? He can mold you, shaping you into a vessel He can use for His Kingdom. No matter how many times that lump of clay—your life—has been molded, or how many times it has fallen apart, God can put you back on His potter's wheel and turn you into a glorious work of art. He'll show you off before the world; you will be a showcase of His glory before the nations. And you will marvel at what God has done to your life as you stay humble in His hands. *That's the key—stay humble.* Stay humble. When you stay humble, God can mold you into the best version of yourself possible.

Now, I want to pray for you, dear reader:

> *Father, in the name of Jesus, I pray for this reader, that the anointing of the Holy Spirit will come into his or her heart and life. Whether on a couch in a living room, at a coffee shop, at a computer, I ask You, Lord, I ask the Holy Spirit to move on this person's life, and that the anointing of God will soar through this reader. Every yoke of bondage will be destroyed, and you will know God in the fullness of His glory.*
>
> *If you're not born again, first and foremost, I pray that you will be saved before you seek the baptism of the Holy Spirit. Repent of your sins and ask the Lord to come into your heart. Then take the next step to receive the baptism of the Holy Spirit. You can lift your hands as I impart the gift of the Holy Spirit to you right now. That anointing of God is coming upon you right now, dear reader.*

When you receive the baptism of Holy Spirit, something may start to bubble up inside you, even around your vocal cords. Don't be afraid that you're not going to speak the right thing or say the wrong thing. Just begin to speak what you feel come up. All of a sudden, at an unknown time, you will begin to speak in your heavenly language. You are receiving a miracle right now in the name of Jesus. I feel the anointing of God right now falling on you. The baptism of the Holy Spirit and the fire has come upon you. He's breaking the spirit of fear and intimidation. Now just receive His gift, simply. All you do is receive. You no longer have to tarry, you can receive it right now, in the blessed name of Jesus Christ of Nazareth. Amen.

God bless you.

PRAYER OF IMPARTATION

Father, in the name of Jesus, we thank you Lord for salvation, first and foremost, being saved by the blood of Jesus. But we realize there is another level beyond salvation. Let us pursue the person of the Holy Spirit. My prayer today is that we not only accept salvation but also pursue the next level in our Christian faith. As we take inventory each day with our walk in God, we cry out in desperation for the closeness of the Holy Spirit's relationship. May we better understand who Christ is in our lives, our families, and our relationships. So, bless everyone this day with a closer walk. In Jesus' name, amen.

Now unto him that is able to do exceedingly abundantly above all that we ask or think, according to the power that worketh in us (Ephesians 3:20 KJV).

3 | WHO IS THE HOLY SPIRIT?

When we have a true understanding of who the Holy Spirit is, learning from the Word of God about the third Person of the Trinity, we can understand the role that the baptism plays in our lives. We need the Holy Spirit and the baptism of fire to accomplish all that God has called us to do.

Approaching the subject of the Holy Spirit inspires the same sacredness as being in the presence of God the Father. Jesus modeled this reverence for us while He was on the earth. In fact, He attributed a greater duty of reverence to the Holy Spirit than even to Himself. He said that it would be forgiven for a person for blaspheming against the Son, but *"Anyone who speaks against the Son of Man can be forgiven, but anyone who speaks against the Holy Spirit will never be forgiven, either in this world or in the world to come"* (Matthew 12:32 NLT).

As believers, we don't have to be intimidated or afraid of blaspheming the Holy Spirit. Only people whose hearts are wicked, not believing anything in the Gospel and refusing to acknowledge and obey God—those are the only ones who may be in danger of blaspheming the Holy Spirit. I've only seen this happen one time in almost thirty years of ministry. So, this is not something we need to feel fear about.

The Holy Spirit should inspire awe, but not fear. He is longing to make Himself known to us. Sometimes people can think of the Holy Spirit as an "it" or a "thing," but the truth is that He is a person. In the Bible, He is addressed as an individual. Through my encounters with the Holy Spirit, He has become more real to me than any other person I know. And these encounters are not rare or hard to achieve. When you pursue a relationship with Him, praying and seeking after God, you can have daily encounters with the third Person of the Trinity. My prayer is that, even as you begin to understand His attributes and character through this teaching, you will encounter the Holy Spirit in a real, life-changing way.

WHO IS HE?

The Holy Spirit is the *third Person of the Godhead, the Trinity: "For there are three that bear witness in heaven: the Father, the Word* [Jesus], *and the Holy Spirit; and these three are one"* (1 John 5:7).

The Holy Spirit is the *authority of God: "And Jesus came and spoke to them, saying, 'All authority has been given to Me in heaven and on earth. Go therefore and make disciples of all the nations, baptizing them in the name of the Father and of the Son and of the Holy Spirit, teaching them to observe all things that I have commanded you; and lo, I am with you always, even to the end of the age.'"* Amen (Matthew 28:18-20).

He is the *compassion of Christ: "When He had been baptized, Jesus came up immediately from the water; and behold, the heavens were opened to Him, and He saw the Spirit of God descending like a dove and alighting upon Him"* (Matthew 3:16).

He is the *breath of life: "The Spirit of God has made me, and the breath of the Almighty gives me life"* (Job 33:4; Genesis 2:7).

The Holy Spirit is *our companion.* A companion is a comrade or a mate, one who walks alongside you.

The Holy Spirit *cares deeply* about you, even if that seems unreal or too good to be true. He is intimately concerned with your life.

He is *God's representative* to all humankind, every single human. In the very beginning, in the Book of Genesis, we read that the Spirit of God was moving upon the face of the water setting the stage for the creation of the world. The Holy Spirit was there during those first steps, working with God to illuminate their divine destiny to humanity

He is the most *gentle* of the Trinity. Even though He's named last in the Trinity—the Father, the Son, the Holy Spirit—they are equal yet with distinct characters. The most gentle one of the three is the Holy Spirit. God is so protective of Him that He warns us to not cross the line when speaking about the Holy Spirit. Nonetheless, we are to seek Him. If you want to get closer to God, seek the Holy Spirit. I often tell people that if they want to see miracles in healing, "Seek the healer, seek God, seek the Holy Spirit and you'll see how quickly the manifestation begins to take place."

The Holy Spirit is the *agent of God*, His revelation and purpose with humankind. Because of the Holy Spirit, we can come to the awareness of who Christ is, and the fullness of His glory for our lives, as recorded in Second Corinthians 5:17: *"Therefore, if anyone is in Christ, he is a new creation; old things have passed away; behold, all things have become new."*

The Holy Spirit *reveals the testimony of Jesus*. Through the Holy Spirit, we have access to the revelation of who God is, who His Son is, and of His purpose and His will for our everyday lives. It is only through the Holy Spirit that you receive revelation. He reveals the testimony of Jesus, the spirit of prophecy.

When you have an encounter with the Holy Spirit and get to know Him more intimately, you'll have such a life-changing walk with Him and a reverence of Him that you will welcome His love, guidance, and even His discipline. In a later chapter, we will discuss the ways you can know Him more intimately and how you can be aware of what may grieve Him. He is The Holy Spirit moves throughout the earth seeking individuals who are calling upon His name. The Old and New Testaments give us many examples of the Holy Spirit intervening and coming upon people in order to manifest God's will upon the earth.

THE ANOINTING OIL

Every one of the examples throughout the Bible when it talks about the Holy Spirit coming upon someone, the person involved was anointed with oil. We see this when the Holy Spirit came upon David in First Samuel 16:13: *"Then Samuel took the horn of oil and anointed him in the midst of his brothers; and the Spirit of the Lord came upon David from that day forward...."* And, suddenly, that little shepherd boy had power over strongholds. Even Goliath, who had paralyzed the whole entire nation of Israel, was no match for God's anointing. When you know the third Person of the Godhead, He will empower you and truly reveal revelation of God through His Word, through prayer, and through fasting.

Oil is the symbol of the Spirit of God. In biblical times, oil was used in every lamp. So, the oil of the Holy Spirit represented the Light of the world. David was anointed by Samuel the prophet with oil, which enabled him, by the Holy Spirit, to conquer the greatest of opposition and the greatest enemy of Israel. In Psalm 23:5, David describes the anointing this way: *"You prepare a table before me in the presence of my enemies; You anoint my head with oil; my cup runs over."* Here, David is speaking of the anointment of the Holy Spirit that enabled him to overcome the giant Goliath.

The fear of Goliath paralyzed the entire camp of Israel, except for the little lad named David, who had a secret. He had a personal relationship with God that had been developed over time. God was his personal Shepherd. David knew God, and God knew David. David also knew that Samuel had anointed him with the oil. Samuel was one of the most feared prophets in the Old Testament: *"So Samuel did what the Lord said, and went to Bethlehem. And the elders of the town trembled at his coming, and said, 'Do you come peaceably?'"* (1 Samuel 16:4). Samuel had an anointment of the Holy Spirit on him—the third Person walked with him.

So, David, being a shepherd and knowing the special anointing upon him, helped his people step into victory over their enemies. His relationship with the Holy Spirit also helped him to understand and step into his role as the future king. Only through the revelation of the Holy Spirit could he have fully understood that.

Like David, the Holy Spirit will reveal to you the role God intended you to fill upon the earth. When you know God personally and develop your relationship with Him, as David did out in the fields with his sheep, you are invited to walk in the favor and miracles of God. From this place of relationship, an understanding of your identity can grow, until you can declare the following with confidence:

> *I am who God says I am. I can do what God says I can do. I can be what God says I can be. Everything in my life is going to be all right. The Holy Spirit is walking with me every day. He takes me by the hand and leads me.*
>
> *God is going to guide me because I've given Him permission to intercede in my life. He has permission to use my life however He sees fits. The Holy Spirit will teach me every day because I give Him permission to take over my life.*

When your spiritual life is ruled by God, you can control your natural life by understanding how to crucify the flesh and submit your will to God's will. True submission comes when you hear the voice of the Holy Spirit. That's how you get promoted to the next level of intimacy with God. Dear reader, if you want to see success in your life, submit to the will of the Father by the Holy Spirit. Christ cannot enter into relationship with humankind until the Holy Spirit has first connected with a sincere seeker.

FELLOWSHIP WITH GOD

First Corinthians 12:3 says: *"Therefore I make known to you that no one speaking by the Spirit of God calls Jesus accursed, and no one can say that Jesus is Lord except by the Holy Spirit."* In order to have fellowship with God, you need to be delivered from your sins. But you can't really be delivered from your sins until there's first a conviction or awareness of your sins. That's what I call the infilling of the Holy Spirit, when the Holy Spirit begins to convict you. Through His conviction, you can find yourself at the foot of the Cross, asking the Lord to come into your life. Only then can you go a step farther and experience the baptism of the Holy Spirit and fire—the fulfillment of which is speaking in a prayer language.

Mary, the mother of Jesus, had the Holy Spirit in her, with her and on her. She housed the presence of God. For the first time in all of eternity, she housed the Lord Jesus Christ in a human body. All God became all Man dwelling in a womb. When Jesus gave His life so that we could be born again, He also opened up the door to the infilling of the Holy Spirit. We get to participate in a relationship with the Holy Spirit where He brings conviction of our sin, and then we can be saved and born again. Once we are born again, we can seek the baptism of the Holy Spirit and its fulfillment, speaking in the tongues of our prayer language. With these, we are able to go farther in our walk with God as the Holy Spirit teaches us and reveals God's will to us.

Connecting and communicating with the Holy Spirit is crucial to our daily walk with God. There isn't one morning I miss talking to Him, telling Him how much I love Him. There are times when I'll sit at the table and even pull out a chair for the Holy Spirit. We sit together and converse about the heavenly Father and about what God wants to do on the earth. Now, this might seem foolish to the natural person, but I live more in the spirit now than I do in the natural.

I didn't get to this place overnight. But through times of fasting and praying, seeking the Holy Spirit, desiring to know Him more intimately and more personally, I've come to realize something. The more I honor the Holy Spirit, the closer I draw to Him. Just because I can't see Him with my natural eyes, does not mean He's not with me. He lets me feel His presence. And this kind of intimacy and closeness is available to everyone.

We can acknowledge and Honor the Holy Spirit even before we are aware of His presence, because, when you've welcomed Him in your life, He's already there. And His presence will be your guide as you walk through your life. Let the Holy Spirit show you what pleases God and what doesn't. Because, in order to have true fellowship with God, we must yield to His will. We must get to a place where we say, "All right, Lord, I yield to Your will, not my will." Remember what Jesus said as He was facing death, "... not what I will, but what You will" (Mark 14:36). Only through the empowerment of the third Person was Jesus able to submit His will onto the Cross.

We have an incredible opportunity to fellowship with the Almighty God in body, soul, and spirit. What an honor, what a conviction, and what a privilege to have. God is living inside you. You are a temple of the Holy Spirit. We get to that privilege and responsibility and reveal the Kingdom of God to the world.

FREE MORAL AGENTS

Humans are free moral agents. What does that mean? That means that God will never violate your will. Because of this, in order to have communion with God, you have to freely choose to yield your will to Him, desiring for the Holy Spirit to take over your life. God is waiting to communicate with you. But you have to be willing to invite Him into your life like you would invite your family at the table to sit down and dine with you. The Holy Spirit is waiting to have that same kind of daily, intimate experience with you. He desires to sit with you probably more than you have a desire to be with Him. Trust me, He's waiting for an invitation from you.

Because we are free moral agents, we can either reject or accept the ruling of the Holy Spirit in our lives. The Holy Spirit is sensitive; He'll woo you or convict you, whichever you need at the moment. But, if we don't yield to Him, heeding His convictions, we risk the possibility of wounding Him. The apostle Paul says in First Thessalonians 5:19, *"Do not quench the Spirit."* The New Living Translation says it this way, *"Do not stifle the Holy Spirit."* These verses seem to reveal that the Holy Spirit has emotions. True friendship means caring about the heart, the emotions of one another.

This means that, when God calls us to do something through His Holy Spirit, we do not refuse His call. Instead, we answer it. I remember, years ago, when I worked in a grocery store. There was a certain man who worked there too. And every day the Lord said to me, "I want you to witness to him."

I asked the Lord, "Every day?"

He replied, "Yes, every day."

So, every single day I walked up to the guy and said, "It's time to get saved. It's time to have the baptism of the Holy Spirit."

And every single day he would just say, "No, I'm not going to church." And he would walk away.

One day I said, "Well, even if you don't go to church, you still need to be saved."

He thought for a minute and said, "Well, I've got to be a good person before I can go to church."

"No," I said, "you don't have to be a good person to go to church." But he refused and went on his way.

So, every day I would witness to him and say, "You need to know that God is ready to do a new thing in your life. If the conviction of the Holy Spirit is not there, there is no way you can turn from your sins. You need to know that. The Holy Spirit is the One who convinces you."

Finally, one day, I looked at the man and said, "I've been coming to you every day for the last several weeks. I'm not asking you to come to church this time. I'm asking you, 'Don't you want to be born again? Don't you want to serve the Lord?'"

He said, "You know what? I'm going to go with you to church on Sunday."

He said this on Friday night, so I said, "You don't need to wait to go to church to get saved or have the Holy Spirit come into your life."

He said, "No, I'm going to wait until Sunday."

On Saturday night, he went out partying like he normally did every Saturday. When he left the bar that night, though, he got on his motorcycle and was involved in a head-on collision. I would never again lay eyes on him. When I heard the news that he had died instantly, I realized how important it was that I had obeyed the Lord. Because of the Holy Spirit's prompting, I had given the man the opportunity to spend eternity in Heaven.

Watch what you say and what you do. Remember, you are the temple, the very residence of the Holy Spirit. When you respond to God's call to follow Him and become one of His children, the Holy Spirit brings your soul into direct fellowship with God. The Spirit is a candle of the Lord, lighting up your way and teaching you every day what pleases Him. All you have to do is seek Him. I've seen too many people walk away from God's leading and refuse the call on their lives. Whatever God calls you to do, He will equip you to do it. You have heavenly backing to fulfill your calling.

THE SPIRIT OF LIFE

This Spirit of God is the new creation we get to participate in when Paul describes our transformation in Second Corinthians 5:17, *"Therefore, if anyone is in Christ, he is a new creation; old things have passed away; behold, all things have become new."* Because of the work of the Holy Spirit in our conversion, many people imagine that conversion is God's ultimate goal. But He had even more in mind for us when He sent His Holy Spirit.

While the Holy Spirit has always been present, there is a distinction between His place of abode before the day of Pentecost and after. Jesus said in John 14, *"the Spirit of truth, whom the world cannot receive, because it neither sees Him nor knows Him; but you know Him, for He dwells with you and will be in you"* (John 14:17). Jesus prophesied that His disciples would be filled with the Holy Spirit after Jesus had gone to Calvary to establish a better covenant. And He was looking forward to the day of Pentecost when the Holy Spirit would actually make His abode within the disciples.

Paul, then, confirmed these truths in First Corinthians 3:16-17 and 6:19-20:

> *Do you not know that **you are the temple of God** and that **the Spirit of God dwells in you?** If anyone defiles the temple of God, God will destroy him. For the temple of God is holy, which temple you are.*
>
> *Or do you not know that **your body is the temple of the Holy Spirit who is in you,** whom you have from God, and you are not your own? For you were bought at a price; therefore glorify God in your body and in your spirit, which are God's.*

We are the temples of the Holy Spirit. This kind of language hadn't been used before. The human body wasn't described as being the dwelling place of the Holy Spirit until the blood of Christ was shed for the sanctification of His people. The human heart was not worthy of the Holy Spirit's entry until it had been truly sanctified by the sacrifice of Jesus.

Oh, my dear reader, we need to live sanctified lives, coming out from among the world! It was upon the death, resurrection, and the glorification of Christ that the Holy Spirit became effective in us. Only after these events were the disciples able to receive the Holy Spirit. Jesus knew that after His departure there would be a need to edify His Church and stimulate its growth. Therefore, the nine gifts of the Spirit were given by the Holy Spirit to accomplish these tasks.

These nine spiritual gifts belong to the Holy Spirit; He imparts them according to God's design and will for His people. We'll talk about those gifts in an upcoming chapter. For now, know that Jesus gave five gifts to the Church: 1) apostle; 2) prophet; 3) evangelist; 4) pastor; and 5) teacher, for the perfecting of the saints and the glory of the Church (see Ephesians 4:11).

The manifestation of these gifts, along with the fruits of the Spirit which the people were to display, allows the Church to represent the Kingdom of God to the world. Galatians 5:22-23 says, *"the fruit of the Spirit is love, joy, peace, longsuffering, kindness, goodness, faithfulness, gentleness, self-control."* People will know who we are by the fruit of our lives, so developing the fruit of the Spirit is vital. We cannot let the anointing carry us where our strength of character cannot keep us.

We, the people of God, are to model His Kingdom through the companionship and the indwelling of the Holy Spirit in our lives. The same Holy Spirit Jesus depended on is ready for you. The same Holy Spirit who gave Jesus the faith He needed during His earthly ministry is prepared to empower you as well.

The Holy Spirit has gifted you with specific gifts that you need to fulfill your specific assignment in God's Kingdom. The Holy Spirit anoints everybody differently, but desires to use everyone for His glory. He may anoint you to be an evangelist, a teacher, or a pastor. Whatever the Holy Spirit calls you to do for the Lord Jesus Christ, accept it and stay in your lane.

One day we had tryouts for the praise team, and this one sweet daughter of the Lord, whom we all love, said she wanted to try out to be a member of the praise team. She sang the song and it sounded worse than the mockingbird. After she was finished, all I could think was, *Well, she's certainly gifted in other areas, but she's not gifted with a pleasant voice.* Focus on what God has called you to do, don't get distracted by other people's callings. Cultivate your gift and release it with your whole heart. Do it unto the Lord, not to please people, and I promise you glory will follow.

Education is wonderful, and, as you pursue your calling, I would encourage you to learn all that you can. However, you need the power of the Holy Spirit to guide you. There are things that secular, or even spiritual, education cannot teach you, but the anointing of the Holy Spirit can. The apostle Paul credited his own outstanding ministry to the great power and demonstration of the Spirit. Even though Paul was trained in the finest of facilities and by the greatest of leadership, he counted it all as garbage compared to living for Christ (Philippians 3:8). He was grateful for the education, but he knew what was truly important.

PRAYER OF IMPARTATION

Father, I pray today, that everyone will discover who the person of the Holy Spirit is as he draws them closer in their relationship with God, revealing Himself as the third person of the Godhead. Even as Job said the breath of God has made me, he realized it was the Holy Spirit that was that breath in our individual lives. I pray, in Jesus' name, that He becomes more real to them than the air that they breathe. Grant this to them I pray, in Jesus' name, amen.

For there are three that bear record in heaven, the Father, the Word, and the Holy Ghost: and these three are one (1 John 5:7 KJV).

4 | RECEIVING THE FATHER'S PROMISE

Yet I dare not boast about anything except what Christ has done through me, bringing the Gentiles to God by my message and by the way I worked among them. They were convinced by the power of miraculous signs and wonders and by the power of God's Spirit. In this way, I have fully presented the Good News of Christ from Jerusalem all the way to Illyricum.
—ROMANS 15:18-19 NLT

In the above verses, the apostle Paul explains how the Gentiles were convinced of the truth of the Gospel by the manifestation of miraculous signs and wonders. You can argue philosophies, tradition, ideologies, whatever the case may be, but no one can argue with a miracle. And no one can do miracles unless God is with them.

God uses humans to do His work among humankind. He is waiting for human instruments to flow through to release His Kingdom on the earth. He flowed through Moses, and now He wants to flow through you. He flowed through Esther, and now He wants to flow through you. He flowed through Abraham, and now He wants to flow through you. He flowed through Deborah, and He's waiting to flow through you to help you carry on the ministry with signs, wonders, and miracles.

First Peter 1:12 says, *"To them it was revealed that, not to themselves, but to us they were ministering the things which now have been reported to you through those who have preached the gospel to you by the Holy Spirit sent from heaven—things which angels desire to look into."* Even the angels want to see how the Holy Spirit is using your life. When you're worshiping God, it gets the attention of all of Heaven. Because, when you are dependent on the Holy Spirit, it changes the atmosphere around you. You create an atmosphere of praise that changes everything about your life.

As humans we have weaknesses and limited abilities. It is only when we are completely dependent on the Holy Spirit that we can rise above our humanity and enter into His strength and capability. Our human strength, our intellect, all of our achievements and accomplishments can only truly be seen through the light of the Holy Spirit. We are nothing apart from our dependency on

Him. He's the one who truly know how to touch our hearts and the heart of the Father.

When we talk about the glory, we're talking about the heart-beat of God, the heart of the Father. The Holy Spirit reveals every beat of the Father's heart. In other words, when you are dependent on the Holy Spirit, your life will reflect the beat of God's heart. Your timing will sync with His plan for your life. Prophesying the infilling of the Holy Spirit at Pentecost, Isaiah 28:11 says, *"For with stammering lips and another tongue He will speak to this people."* God wants to speak to you through the Holy Spirit. Are you ready?

RECEIVING THE FIRE

Now that you understand who the Holy Spirit is, the next thing we will discuss is how you can receive the baptism of the Holy Spirit and fire. To the best of my ability, I'm going to teach you how to receive the promise of the Father.

As it was ordained of God for the disciples of Jesus to be baptized in Holy Spirit, so it is God's divine purpose and plan for every born-again believer to receive the same blessing from Jesus. While Jesus was on earth He declared, *"I will pray the Father, and He will give you another Helper, that He may abide with you forever— the Spirit of truth, whom the world cannot receive, because it neither sees Him nor knows Him; but you know Him, for He dwells with you and will be in you"* (John 14:16-17). One of the last statements Jesus made before ascending to Heaven refers to the blessed baptism and the Holy Spirit.

He instructed His followers to, *"...wait for the Promise of the Father, 'which,' He said, 'you have heard from Me; for John truly baptized with water, but you shall be baptized with the Holy Spirit not many days from now'"* (Acts 1:4-5). The same reason that made it essential for the early believers to be baptized with the Holy Spirit applies to each one of us today.

This experience is essential to our own benefit and welfare. Jesus says in John 16:7, *"...It is to your advantage that I go away; for if I do not go away, the Helper will not come to you; but if I depart, I will send Him to you."* Jesus knew that His departure meant that the third Person of the Trinity would come down and dwell in the bodies of faithful believers to be a Comforter, a Friend, and a Guide. The Holy Spirit is our gift from the Father no matter where we go or what hardships we walk through. Just like in David's Psalm 23, it matters not how difficult life may appear to be at times, He is always present as an intimate Companion and Counselor.

The Holy Spirit is our Teacher (Luke 12:12; John 14:26). He is our Guide into all truth (John 16:13). He brings us peace, joy, and hope. That's why I told the story of the dear woman trying out for the praise team. God knew she had received a great gift from Him, but singing was not it. She always smiled and had a way of bringing joy to people. Likewise, your smile may be one of your gifts. Whatever you do to help lighten somebody's load and put a smile on someone's face leads people closer to the Lord. Whether it is being a bold witness or listening to others with compassion, the Holy Spirit leads and guides you to release your gift to the world.

Remember, the Holy Spirit wants you to have joy, hope, and peace that surpasses all understanding (Romans 14:17; 15:13). He makes our prayers effective and gives us direct communication with the Father. You can dialogue with God (Romans 8:26-27). Even when we don't know how to pray, He knows how to pray with groanings and utterances that we cannot interpret when praying in the Holy Spirit. When you receive your prayer language and start praying in tongues, your life begins to change. Everything about you—your ministry, your family, your marriage, your occupation, etc.—will change for the better when you start praying in the Spirit.

I learned years ago that one of the greatest keys for accessing the realms of miracles was spending time praying in tongues. The Holy Spirit molds and develops the character of the person in whom He abides in such a way as to reflect His own character. Again, character is essential for the anointing. Many times, we get caught up in the anointing so that we forget to work on our character too. I just don't look for the anointing when I visit churches or I stand with evangelists at revivals—I look for character, for the fruit of the Spirit to be manifest in their lives.

I've seen many people with anointing, but no character. You need to see both components taking place in the life of the individual to know that God is really working His plan in that individual. Both components are essential for the Holy Spirit to use because He wants you to reflect God on earth. So, your character matters if you're going to represent God accurately. As the Bible says, *"the fruit of the Spirit is love, joy, peace, longsuffering, gentleness, goodness, faithfulness, gentleness, and self-control."* We all have to mature in our faith. And nothing helps us to grow in maturity more than yielding to the Holy Spirit.

KEYS TO RECEIVING THE BAPTISM OF THE HOLY SPIRIT

Below, I have listed several keys to help you, as a believer, to receive the baptism of the Holy Spirit. Some I'll elaborate on more than others, but all the keys are essential to receiving the baptism of the Holy Spirit.

Salvation

The first key is salvation. No one can receive the baptism of the Holy Spirit or know the third Person of the Holy Spirit intimately, without being born again. The Holy Spirit convicts you of your sins or your wrongdoing. He introduces you to Jesus. Therefore, you receive Jesus as your Lord and Savior, and you have what is called the *infilling* of the Spirit. But you don't have the baptism—the *fulfilling* of the Spirit—yet, praying in the prayer language or speaking in tongues. So, the first key is recognizing you're born again. According to Second Corinthians 5:17, you become a new creature: *"Therefore, if anyone is in Christ, he is a new creation; old things have passed away; behold, all things have become new."* And Jesus says in John 3:3, *"Jesus answered and said to him, 'Most assuredly, I say to you, unless one is born again, he cannot see the kingdom of God.'"*

Surrender and Yield

The next key is surrendering and yielding yourself to God. When you surrender to God, you yield yourself to Him. The apostle Paul wrote to the Galatians, *"I have been crucified with Christ; it is no longer I who live, but Christ lives in me; and the life which I now live in the flesh I live by faith in the Son of God, who loved me and gave*

Himself for me." The more you surrender and the more you yield your will to His will, the easier it is to see Him in your life as your Helper and Guide. As you surrender daily, allowing God to strip away anything inside of you that He doesn't like, the more He is able to pour out His goodness and blessings on you. There has to be a willingness on your part; He will not force Himself on you. He will not validate *your* will. You must desire *His* will.

Seek

The third key is seeking. Remember, God wants you to have this empowering experience. He is not hiding this baptism of fire from you. It's His desire that the Holy Spirit would come in and dwell in the temple of your body. But your attitude is important. It is your attitude that determines the altitude. How high you really want to go with God all depends on your attitude. When you adjust your attitude, you will find that the Lord will give to you generously. John 21:1-12 tells of the time when Jesus told Simon Peter to let his nets fall into the water on the right side of the boat. Simon Peter was reluctant to do so because he and the others had been fishing all night and they "caught nothing." If he would have allowed his natural senses and human emotions to rule, Simon Peter would not have followed Jesus' instructions. But, because he did what Jesus said, he experienced the supernatural: *"they were unable to haul the net in because of the large number of fish. …Simon Peter climbed back into the boat and dragged the net ashore. It was full of large fish, 153, but even with so many the net was not torn."*

Jesus says in Matthew 7:7-8: *"Ask, and it will be given to you; seek, and you will find; knock, and it will be opened to you. For everyone who asks receives, and he who seeks finds, and to him who knocks it will be opened."* So, are you ready to seek? Are you ready to ask? Are you ready to knock with the right attitude? When you seek you will find Him. *"If a son asks for bread from any father among you, will he give him a stone?"* (Luke 11:11). Of course not. You wouldn't give your hungry child a loaf of stone to make a bologna sandwich. Never. So how much more will God honor you and give you the desires of your heart and the baptism of the Holy Spirit?

The results of having faith in God is found in Mark 11:24. Jesus says, *"Therefore I say to you, whatever things you ask when you pray, believe that you receive them, and you will have them."* Again, Hebrews confirms what our faith means to God, *"But without faith it is impossible to please Him, for he who comes to God must believe that He is, and that He is a rewarder of those who diligently seek Him."*

Obedience

Another key is obedience. First Samuel 15:22 says that *"to obey is better than sacrifice."* If you're willing and obedient, not only shall you eat the good of the land, but you shall have the fullness of the Godhead.

Fasting

The fifth key is fasting, which is very important. Understand this: prayer produces the power, but fasting crucifies your flesh. God ordains fasting so you can submit your will to His will. Fasting is mentioned in the Bible about a third as many times as prayer. That's how important fasting is. There are examples of fasting by almost every man and woman of God in the Bible: Elijah fasted forty days. Daniel fasted for twenty-one days. David fasted. Esther and her people fasted. Jesus fasted forty days and forty nights.

Scientifically, your body can go three days without any food and three days without water. Although fasting is essential and powerful, it would not be wise for a beginner to try a forty day fast. Fasting can also be dangerous for your physical health, so be cautious and start slowly. If fasting isn't wise for your overall health, consider giving up something else that means something to you. Fasting is not about starving yourself; it is about positioning yourself in a posture of sacrifice.

If you're healthy enough to fast food, though, I would encourage you to do that. I've been around many people who have fasted for forty days. Personally, I've done both long and short fasts. It is an incredibly powerful experience. It clears your mind, submitting your will to God's will, which results clearly hearing the Holy Spirit speak about people, world events, etc. If you are a mature Christian with years of studying the Word and walking with the Lord, this is not news to you.

However, if you haven't fasted before, my advice is that you begin with a half-day fast. For example, fast a breakfast one day. Then the next week fast breakfast and lunch. Start building yourself up daily so you can fast two meals a week. After that, you will have established a habit of fasting. And when you have a habit of fasting, you can take on more levels of fasting. Over the years, many people have said to me, "I prayed and fasted but the first day nothing happened and the second day nothing happened."

I tell them, "Well, keep pursuing. Keep pressing in. Because the more you yield yourself to Him, believe me He's going to fill you with the Holy Spirit. You're going to be baptized and begin speaking in tongues." The 120 believers in the upper room fasted for ten days while waiting for their baptism of the Holy Spirit. And the fire of the Holy Spirit fell on all of them.

WHY DO YOU NEED THE HOLY SPIRIT BAPTISM?

To Serve Others

The Holy Spirit will empower you from on high to serve others. The Holy Spirit will teach you how to serve more effectively. Serving is a key that unlocks one of the greatest realms of glory I've ever seen God unlock. I asked God, "I know I can serve others, but why do I need the baptism of the Holy Spirit to do that?" He revealed to me that the Holy Spirit uses us as instruments to bring salvation, healing, and blessing to the world through the Gospel. When we look at the disciples, we can see the great transformation that the Holy Spirit worked in their lives for the effective purpose of revealing the good news of Jesus Christ. After the disciples received the Holy Spirit, they became courageous, steadfast, and willing to lay down their lives.

To Boldly Preach the Good News of Jesus

Simon Peter denied the Lord Jesus three times after Jesus was arrested. But, after the upper room Pentecost experience, he was as bold and strong as a lion. The Bible says to come boldly to the throne of grace (Hebrews 4:16) and before God—be bold as a lion, attaining the power and authority. Peter was transformed after he received the baptism of the Holy Spirit. He stood before multitudes proclaiming the good news of Jesus Christ, the Messiah. Jesus speaks of this transforming power of the Holy Spirit when He said to His followers that they would receive power after the Holy Spirit comes upon you.

To Be an Effective Witness

If you want to be an effective witness, you need the baptism of the Holy Spirit. You cannot be an effective witness without Him. If you have been anointed by the Holy Spirit, you will notice that people will even begin to be convicted in your presence.

To Receive Power

Jesus said to His followers that they would receive power after the Holy Spirit comes upon them and be witnesses to Him both in Jerusalem and to the utmost parts of the earth (Acts 1:8).

To Receive Spiritual Gifts

There are various spiritual gifts cited in First Corinthians 12:4-11 that we will be discussing in the next chapter. You are blessed with these spiritual gifts so you can be used by God to further His Kingdom. These gifts should not make you high-minded or prideful. Those who are truly being used by God recognize that their gifting does not come from themselves, but entirely from God. Keep that key thought in your mind while you also realize that it is the Lord's will that we covet the best gifts (see 1 Corinthians 12:31).

I hope when reading this chapter that you have been encouraged to go after the Holy Spirit—that you now know who He is as a person. The Holy Spirit has feelings just as you and I do. We don't want to grieve His feelings. He deserves the utmost respect, but we don't need to be fearful of Him. He is gentle and wants to walk with us through our lives, moment by moment.

I'd like to pray over you:

> *Father, in the name of Jesus, thank You for this teaching, this revelation of who the Holy Spirit is and how we can receive the baptism of the Holy Spirit. We know now how we can be effective witnesses and walk in authority. We know what the prerequisites are to receiving the baptism of Your Holy Spirit. We will place You in our everyday lives as we walk as adventurers of faith, as Christian believers of the Gospel. Father, I pray for this reader and all readers of this book and thank you right now that the Holy Spirit is touching each one from the crown of their head to the soles of their feet. He's anointing you with power and authority, and you want to be used by God. It is Your desire, it is Your will, Lord, that this person will be filled and baptized with the Holy Spirit. Amen.*

I break every spirit of fear every spirit of intimidation from you, dear reader. God is waiting for you. He's waiting as the third Person for your invitation to come and sit with you, to talk with you, to guide you. Why don't you invite Him now? That's my prayer for you today. To invite the Holy Spirit as the third Person gratefully into your life, thanking Him for introducing you to Christ—because without Him, you don't really know Christ.

God bless you.

Prayer of Impartation

Father, I pray in Jesus' name, that the promises of the Holy Spirit, the baptism of the Holy Spirit will come upon your child now. As it speaks in Acts 1:8, you shall receive power after the Holy Spirit comes upon you. I pray this so that they shall be effective in their calling from you. I ask that they receive the promise of the Holy Ghost this day in their lives. In Jesus' name, amen.

But ye shall receive power, after that the Holy Ghost is come upon you: and ye shall be witnesses unto me both in Jerusalem, and in all Judaea, and in Samaria, and unto the uttermost part of the earth (Acts 1:8 KJV).

5 | THE NINE GIFTS OF THE HOLY SPIRIT

There are diversities of gifts, but the same Spirit. There are differences of ministries, but the same Lord. And there are diversities of activities, but it is the same God who works all in all. But the manifestation of the Spirit is given to each one for the profit of all: for to one is given the word of wisdom through the Spirit, to another the word of knowledge through the same Spirit, to another faith by the same Spirit, to another gifts of healings by the same Spirit, to another the working of miracles, to another prophecy, to another discerning of spirits, to another different kinds of tongues, to another the interpretation of tongues. But one and the same Spirit works all these things, distributing to each one individually as He wills.

—1 CORINTHIANS 12:4-11

*T*his important chapter discusses the nine gifts of the Holy Spirit and the heavenly keys to unlocking and accessing your spiritual gifts. My hope is that you would have a clear understanding of each gift and learn how they can operate in your life and define your purpose, glorifying the Father according to God's will.

First Corinthians 14:12 says, *"Even so you, since you are zealous for spiritual gifts, let it be for the edification of the church that you seek to excel."*

And Ephesians 4:11-13 says of Jesus and the gifts:

> *He Himself gave some to be apostles, some prophets, some evangelists, and some pastors and teachers, **for the equipping of the saints for the work of ministry, for the edifying of the body of Christ**, till we all come to the unity of the faith and of the knowledge of the Son of God, to a perfect man, to the measure of the stature of the fullness of Christ.*

Let's take a deep dive into the opening Scripture passage from First Corinthians 12. First Corinthians 12:8-10 says:

> *For to one is given the **word of wisdom** through the Spirit, to another the **word of knowledge** through the same spirit, to another **faith** by the same spirit, to another **gifts of healings** by the same Spirit, to another the **working of miracles**, to another **prophecy**, to another **discerning of spirits**, to another **different kinds of tongues**, to another the **interpretation of tongues**.*

The spiritual gifts are distinct from the office of the fivefold ministry—apostles, prophets, evangelists, pastors, and teachers. The fivefold ministry is the administration that God set up for the Church as a way to empower His Body in the operation of the gifts. The nine gifts of the Spirit, then, operate through God's people as instruments for His use. All of these gifts work together by the Holy Spirit; whatever need there is at any given time, He'll present the gift to the individual to meet that need.

THREE GIFT CATEGORIES

The spiritual gifts fall into three categories according to their purpose: *revelation, inspiration, and power.* And within each of these three categories, there are three distinct gifts. Organizing the spiritual gifts would look something like this:

Revelation

- Word of Wisdom
- Word of Knowledge
- Discerning of Spirits

Inspiration

- Different Tongues
- Interpretation of Tongues
- Prophecy

Power

- Working of Miracles
- Faith

- Gifts of Healings

Now let's delve right into the first category of spiritual gifts. You will be amazed at how generous the Holy Spirit wants to be with you!

REVELATION GIFTS

The first category is revelation, and, within that category, the three gifts are:

1. Word of wisdom
2. Word of knowledge
3. Discerning of spirits

I've been asked this question many times, "Can everyone operate in the gifts of Spirit?" And my answer is always, "Yes, certainly, every believer may operate in one or more of the gifts of the Spirit."

There are two purposes for spiritual gifts: to glorify the Father and to edify the Church. The verse we looked at earlier points to this holy purpose. In Ephesians 4:12 (KJV), it says, *"For the perfecting of the saints, for the work of the ministry, for the edifying of the body of Christ."* This is why the gifts are set in place by the Holy Spirit for believers.

Word of Wisdom Gift

The first gift in the Revelation category is the word of wisdom. This gift is given by the Spirit of God to each believer who seeks it. The apostle Paul says in First Corinthians 14:12 that we are to be zealous for spiritual gifts. When you seek the gifts of the Holy

Spirit, you seek the Holy Spirit; He's the Giver. He will operate through those gifts according to your desire and the mandate and calling on your life.

The word of wisdom gift is the supernatural revelation of the divine purpose of God implanted or revealed to believers. With this gift, the Spirit of God chooses to release God's wisdom about a future circumstance, the cause of a situation, or answers to a problem. First Corinthians 2:7 says, *"But we speak the wisdom of God in a mystery, the hidden wisdom which God ordained before the ages for our glory."* God's wisdom is imparted to a person at the moment the Spirit of God flows through the individual to speak. With this gift, it is as though God is speaking His wisdom for the future through the mouthpiece of a human.

Jesus predicted the future. He said that false christs and messiahs would come, that there would be wars and rumors of wars, that there would be famines, pestilence, and earthquakes. He also said there would be great tribulation such as the world had never seen. The sun would be darkened, and the moon would not shine (Matthew 24:5-28). And in Matthew 24:30, Jesus said, *"Then the sign of the Son of Man will appear in the heaven...and they will see the Son of Man coming on the clouds of heaven with power and great glory."* Jesus was predicting or projecting the future not as God, but as an anointed man through whom the gift of the word of wisdom flowed. And the same Holy Spirit that operated in Jesus' earthly ministry wants to operate in you.

When we examine Jesus' earthly ministry, we see He had extraordinary faith, which He demonstrated in His lifestyle of prayer. He dialogued continually with His heavenly Father. When you are in constant conversation with God, you will be more sensitive to the direction that the Holy Spirit is leading you, becoming more and more aware of how He wants to reveal God's glory through your life.

The word of wisdom gift is supernatural—not a natural talent—born from your spiritual birth. The gifts are not a skill you are taught. They are something you seek and receive from the Holy Spirit Himself. The third Person of the Trinity gives and operates in these gifts as He sees fit to meet the present needs of the world.

Jesus spoke about the future, predicting what was going to come to those who were listening, sharing God's wisdom so we would be prepared for the last days. The word of wisdom gift has nothing to do with the foolish wisdom of the world. God's wisdom shines a light into the believer—a wisdom that is unknown until the Spirit of God reveals it to you. When the word of wisdom operates through you, it brings solutions to whatever problem it faces. That is how you know the word of wisdom is in operation.

There are examples of this gift operating in the Old Testament. In fact, seven of the nine gifts of the Holy Spirit are in operation throughout the Old Testament. At Pentecost, though, two new gifts were given to the believers: speaking in tongues and the interpretation of tongues.

Today this gift of the word of wisdom is in operation in the lives of not only the prophets, but of all believers. It is one of the most important gifts of the Spirit, because it not only brings the demonstration of God, but it practically resolves problems in people's lives. First Corinthians 12:31 says, *"But earnestly desire the best gifts....*" So, the apostle Paul encourages us to seek the gifts, the revelation gifts especially.

Revelation gifts reveal something that must be discovered. Many people think the Book of Revelation in the Bible is a book of mysteries. No, it's not. God wants us to understand the revelation of who He is through prophecy. He never gave us anything in His Word that He didn't want us to discover about Him. So, the Book of Revelation means to reveal or uncover so you can understand who Christ is and the fullness of His glory.

The prophet Isaiah operated in the word of wisdom gift and prophesied from that gift. He foresaw the future to reveal the coming Messiah as told in Isaiah 9:6-7. His words also foreshadowed the crucified Lord and Savior in Isaiah 53:1-12. Two thousand years before Christ's birth, death, and resurrection, Isaiah unfolded the entire story of the Son of God, even how His torture would be our healing. When we look at the front of the Cross of Jesus, we see God's desire for our sins to be forgiven. But, from the back of the Cross, we see God's desire for us to be healed of all of our sins, sickness, and disease. When we see the Cross, we see our salvation as well as a place of healing, all because of Jesus' sacrifice.

It is my desire in this teaching that, when you read the Bible—the New Testament as well as the Old Testament—you would be able to recognize which gift of the Holy Spirit is in operation. As you become more familiar with the gifts in Scripture, you can start to identify what gift is operating in your ministry or your life as a believer today.

Let's look at another example, in First Kings 3:16-27, of the word of wisdom gift in action.

> Now two women who were harlots came to the king, and stood before him. And one woman said, "O my lord, this woman and I dwell in the same house; and I gave birth while she was in the house. Then it happened, the third day after I had given birth, that this woman also gave birth. And we were together; no one was with us in the house, except the two of us in the house. And this woman's son died in the night, because she lay on him. So she arose in the middle of the night and took my son from my side, while your maidservant slept, and laid him in her bosom, and laid her dead child in my bosom. And when I rose in the morning to nurse my son, there he was, dead. But when I had examined him in the morning, indeed, he was not my son whom I had borne."
>
> Then the other woman said, "No! But the living one is my son, and the dead one is your son."
>
> And the first woman said, "No! But the dead one is your son, and the living one is my son."
>
> Thus they spoke before the king.
>
> And the king said, "The one says, 'This is my son, who lives, and your son is the dead one'; and the other says, 'No! But your son is the dead one, and my son is the living one.'" Then the king said, "Bring me a sword." So they brought a sword before the king. And the king

said, "Divide the living child in two, and give half to one, and half to the other."

Then the woman whose son was living spoke to the king, for she yearned with compassion for her son; and she said, "O my lord, give her the living child, and by no means kill him!"

But the other said, "Let him be neither mine nor yours, but divide him."

So the king answered and said, "Give the first woman the living child, and by no means kill him; she is his mother."

Without God's wisdom, knowledge will bring you no understanding. The Bible says in Hosea 4:6, *"My people are destroyed for lack of knowledge."* We see in this story that Solomon wasn't merely filled with knowledge. He was operating in the Holy Spirit's gift of the word of wisdom. It took only one divine revelation of the word of wisdom to solve the problem. There was no way to naturally discern who the true mother was, but through the supernatural gift, he was able to return the child to its mother and expose the deception of the enemy.

Genesis 6:12-13 is another example. Through the word of wisdom, Noah received a divine revelation of the purpose of God to prepare his household for deliverance. God was going to destroy the whole earth by a flood. With this revelation, Noah was able to prepare the ark according to a word of wisdom. God gave Noah the blueprint and he built the ark. The word of wisdom operated through him, and the ark was God's deliverance—a type of the Cross.

The Holy Spirit conveys this gift in more than just one practical way, as we see in the lives of believers such as Joseph. At age 17, God showed Joseph his predestined purpose through the gift for the word of wisdom in a dream (Genesis 37:2-7). Daniel had a vision of future revelation too (Daniel 1:17). These were words of wisdom gifts operating through these individuals. John the Revelator is given the book of prophecy revealing the end-time prophetic vision, the testimony of Christ, the Spirit of prophecy which is his testimony. And Job foresaw a coming revival that would eventually come upon all of the righteousness of God. These are just a few of the many examples of the gift of word of wisdom throughout the Bible.

As you read God's Word, you can recognize this particular gift in the way that it brings a solution to a problem. In your own life, you will begin to notice moments when you suddenly have an answer to an issue that has been troubling you. It's almost as if the solution is dropped into your spirit to resolve a particular matter at a particular moment in time.

A word of wisdom is distinct from prophecy, though. The word of wisdom resolves a matter and prophecy comforts, consoles. The gift of prophecy, on its own, has no element of revelation. First Corinthians 14:3 says, *"But he who prophesies speaks edification and exhortation and comfort to men."* In other words, you comfort yourself and others when you prophesy. An example of this might be when somebody lays hands on you and says, "The Lord says that He will encourage your heart. You are to fear not, fret not. You shall overcome this situation." That's the gift of prophecy; it has no element of revelation. It didn't reveal the depth of the matter or a practical solution. We'll talk further about prophetic gifting, and others, in the coming pages.

Word of Knowledge Gift

The second gift in the revelation category is the word of knowledge imparted by the Holy Spirit. The word of knowledge is God's knowledge imparted as a word to a believer to reveal the hidden fact of a matter. A word of knowledge can reveal something in someone's past that God wants them to release. Or, it can reveal something in the present. Either way, it shows you something that was hidden from human knowledge.

How can you know this word of knowledge gifting is operating in your life? You may perceive things by the Holy Spirit that reveal a perspective that is different from what is apparent in the natural realm. This perspective can help to bring understanding to the truth of a problem or facilitate a solution. So, whenever you receive a word of wisdom, you commonly will receive the word of knowledge as well. They're almost twins, back to back. Similar to how, when you see someone who operates in the office of a pastor, you almost always see a prophet as well.

There are many examples in the Old Testament of the gift of words of knowledge in operation, including Second Kings:

> But Gehazi, the servant of Elisha the man of God, said, "Look, my master has spared Naaman this Syrian, while not receiving from his hands what he brought; but as the Lord lives, I will run after him and take something from him." So Gehazi pursued Naaman. When Naaman saw him running after

him, he got down from the chariot to meet him, and said, "Is all well?"

And he said, "All is well. My master has sent me, saying, 'Indeed, just now two young men of the sons of the prophets have come to me from the mountains of Ephraim. Please give them a talent of silver and two changes of garments.'"

So Naaman said, "Please, take two talents." And he urged him, and bound two talents of silver in two bags, with two changes of garments, and handed them to two of his servants; and they carried them on ahead of him. When he came to the citadel, he took them from their hand, and stored them away in the house; then he let the men go, and they departed. Now he went in and stood before his master. Elisha said to him, "Where did you go, Gehazi?"

And he said, "Your servant did not go anywhere."

Then he said to him, "Did not my heart go with you when the man turned back from his chariot to meet you? Is it time to receive money and to receive cloth-ing, olive groves and vineyards, sheep and oxen, male and female servants? Therefore the leprosy of Naaman shall cling to you and your descendants for-ever." And he went out from his presence leprous, as white as snow (2 Kings 5:20-27; see also 2 Kings 6).

In the New Testament, Jesus Christ Himself operates in this gift as seen in John 4:16-18:

Jesus said to her, "Go, call your husband, and come here." The woman answered and said, "I have no husband." Jesus said to her, "You have well said, 'I have no husband,' for you have had five husbands, and the one whom you now have is not your husband; in that you spoke truly."

When Jesus spoke to the woman at the well, He was revealing something hidden, something He could not have known naturally. As we see from the woman's stunned reaction to Jesus knowing about her past, a word of knowledge is a tremendous gift. It reveals God's intimate knowledge of each of His children and, when you see this gift in operation, I promise that your life will never be the same. When you come into the presence of the Holy Spirit when He's manifesting His gifts, it will forever bring you into the glory realm where you can see God's hands at work. When we talk about His hands, we're talking about His demonstration of power. When we talk about His heart, we're talking about His glory. When we see God move through the gifts like word of knowledge, we can see as aspect of His divinity revealed.

Let's look at another example, apostle Peter. Matthew 16:13-17 says:

When Jesus came into the region of Caesarea Philippi, He asked His disciples, saying, "Who do men say that I, the Son of Man, am?" So they said, "Some say John the Baptist, some Elijah, and others Jeremiah or one of the prophets." He said to them, "But who do you say that I am?" Simon Peter answered and said, "You are the Christ, the Son of the living God." Jesus answered

> *and said to him, "Blessed are you, Simon Bar-Jonah, for **flesh and blood has not revealed this to you, but My Father who is in heaven**."*

After Peter said that Jesus was the Christ, Jesus told Peter that he received that revelation from God—a word of knowledge—which will unlock certain keys in his life. Jesus continues:

> *I also say to you that you are Peter, and on this rock I will build My church, and the gates of Hades shall not prevail against it. And **I will give you the keys of the kingdom of heaven**, and whatever you bind on earth will be bound in heaven, and whatever you loose on earth will be loosed in heaven* (Matthew 16:18-19).

Christ prophesied over Peter that he would be the foundation of God's Church. In this example, we can see the word of wisdom and prophecy operating together in one passage of Scripture. Jesus reveals revelation to him, shedding light into Peter's life in ministry. Then, He acknowledged that God revealed the truth to Peter supernaturally. He goes on to tell us through prophecy that the gates of hell shall not prevail against the Church.

We get to participate in the victory of Christ. No matter what you go through in this life, the Holy Spirit is alongside to aid you, help you, equip you, carry you, and lead you by the hand to get closer to God. The gift of word of knowledge operating the ministry of the Lord Jesus Christ can be seen in John 1:45-50:

> *Philip found Nathanael and said to him, "We have found Him of whom Moses in the law, and also the prophets, wrote—Jesus of Nazareth, the son of*

Joseph." And Nathanael said to him, "Can anything good come out of Nazareth?" Philip said to him, "Come and see." Jesus saw Nathanael coming toward Him, and said of him, "Behold, an Israelite indeed, in whom is no deceit!" Nathanael said to Him, "How do You know me?" Jesus answered and said to him, "Before Philip called you, when you were under the fig tree, I saw you." Nathanael answered and said to Him, "Rabbi, You are the Son of God! You are the King of Israel!" Jesus answered and said to him, "Because I said to you, 'I saw you under the fig tree,' do you believe? You will see greater things than these."

I've seen this in my own ministry, my own life. People unfamiliar with the spiritual gifts often say, "Cooke, you're psychic. You must have fortune-tellers. How do you know this? How do you know that?" Well, I am no psychic and I don't consult fortune-tellers—heaven forbid! What I do have is the Holy Spirit living within me. I depend totally on Him to anoint me with His gifts as He wills.

There was a man named William Branham. At age 17, he laid hands on one of my mentors who then laid hands on my wife and me, passing the gift to us. After that, we began to operate with the word of knowledge.

I remember being with Brother R. W. Schambach who also laid hands on me, imparting gifts of healings and miracles. Since then, I've seen so many extraordinary, supernatural occurrences. The last thing he told me was, "Carry the fire of God, carry the glory, the gifts, the powers of miracles." God wants to equip each of us for the end-time harvest, and what better way to equip us but through the gifts of the Holy Spirit. The Holy Spirit is waiting to impart those gifts to you for the glory of God.

When Jesus first saw Nathanael, He immediately received a word of knowledge about him. He said, "Here truly is an Israelite in whom there is no deceit" (John 1:47). Nathanael was surprised! In so many words, he asked Jesus, "How do you know? How can You call me a good man?" Supernaturally, the Lord Jesus Christ had seen Nathanael the day before sitting under a fig tree. Just hearing this word of knowledge made a believer out of Nathanael and he said, "Rabbi, You are the Son of God; you are the king of Israel" (John 1:49). Why? Because the gift of word of knowledge had revealed to Jesus Nathanael's whereabouts.

Nathanael was astonished by Jesus' word of knowledge. Jesus said to him, *"Because I said to you, 'I saw you under the fig tree,' do you believe? You will see greater things than these."* I believe the greatest dispensation of God's glory is in the stages now for manifestation. You have to know who you are in God, who God is in you. You are actually the physical address of God. So, get ready; let God prepare you. Get at the foot of the altar, crucify your flesh, let the Holy Spirit come on you, and you will see greater things!

Discerning of Spirits Gift

The last gift of the revelation gifts is the gift of discerning of spirits. Notice that it's called the gift of discerning of spirits, not the discerning of people. This gift does not mean judging people. Sometimes people have said to me, "Well, I just don't like this person and I believe I have a gift for discerning of spirits, so something must be wrong." To which I say, "No, you don't have the gift of discerning of spirits. You're discerning the person, which has nothing to do with the gift of the Holy Spirit."

Discerning of spirits gives you insight into the spiritual world. This gift is also not called the gift of discerning devils. It's discerning the spiritual world. So, operating in this gift means that you can have an angelic revelation. Jacob saw angels ascending and descending from heaven. With this gift, you can discern activity going on in the spirit realm. You can feel and sense things from heaven, but also things that just don't feel right—that's the gift of discerning of spirits. You may come into an atmosphere where your spirit is uneasy or you all of a sudden feel oppressed. That's the gift of discerning spirits operating in your life.

Exodus 33:18-23 describes a conversation between Moses and God:

> *And he [Moses] said, "Please, show me Your glory." Then He said, "I will make all My goodness pass before you, and I will proclaim the name of the Lord before you. I will be gracious to whom I will be gracious, and I will have compassion on whom I will have compassion." But He said, "You cannot see My face; for no man shall see Me, and live." And the Lord said, "Here is a place by Me, and you shall stand on the rock. So it shall be, while My glory passes by, that I will put you in the cleft of the rock, and will cover you with My hand while I pass by. Then I will take away My hand, and you shall see My back; but My face shall not be seen."*

No one will see God's glory until we're in Heaven itself. I'm convinced of that. It's impossible for us to see the face of God while we're living in these earthly vessels. We are not yet perfected. Every day, we have to crucify the flesh, put off the old nature, and put on the new nature. We have to daily take up our cross. But at times we can touch realms of glory, which are phenomenal. God allowed Moses a glimpse into the supernatural realm of glory.

This gift also reveals the spiritual reality behind a supernatural manifestation, whether it is good or evil. Acts 16:16-19 tells of a girl who was possessed with a spirit of divination:

> Now it happened, as we went to prayer, that a certain slave **girl possessed with a spirit of divination** met us, who brought her masters much profit by fortune-telling. This girl followed Paul and us, and cried out, saying, "These men are the servants of the Most High God, who proclaim to us the way of salvation." And this she did for many days. But Paul, greatly annoyed, turned and **said to the spirit, "I command you in the name of Jesus Christ to come out of her." And he came out that very hour.** But when her masters saw that their hope of profit was gone, they seized Paul and Silas and dragged them into the market-place to the authorities.

Through the gift of discerning of spirits, Paul discerned that the girl had an evil spirit. He then dealt with the spirit, not the person. This gift is not a gift of fault finding. We are commanded to *"Be kind to one another, tenderhearted, forgiving one another, even as God in Christ forgave you"* (Ephesians 4:33).

God will not put His gifts and His anointing on anyone who is self-righteous or arrogant. We have to be completely dependent upon the Holy Spirit in order for Him to operate through us. Any extraordinary gifting is entirely because of Him, not us. So, when God uses you, stay humble and give Him all the glory. And when He gets all the glory, He will take you to spectacular realms of glory. Submitted to Him, you will go from glory to glory, faith to faith.

PRAYER OF IMPARTATION

Father, in the name of Jesus, I pray that every person that has read this chapter will begin to receive and understand one of the gifts, if not more than one, to operate in their life and ministry to effectively touch and to minister to the broken, the hurt, and the despondent. Let this show forth Christ and may He be made known through these gifts of the Holy Spirit. My prayer today is that they will desire and seek after the Holy Spirit and what gift they would work in ministry. In Jesus' name, amen.

For to one is given by the Spirit the word of wisdom; to another the word of knowledge by the same Spirit; To another faith by the same Spirit; to another the gifts of healing by the same Spirit; To another the working of miracles; to another prophecy; to another discerning of spirits; to another divers kinds of tongues; to another the interpretation of tongues (1 Corinthians 12:8-10 KJV).

6 | THE NINE GIFTS OF THE HOLY SPIRIT, CONTINUED

There are diversities of gifts, but the same Spirit. There are differences of ministries, but the same Lord. And there are diversities of activities, but it is the same God who works all in all. But the manifestation of the Spirit is given to each one for the profit of all: for to one is given the word of wisdom through the Spirit, to another the word of knowledge through the same Spirit, to another faith by the same Spirit, to another gifts of healings by the same Spirit, to another the working of miracles, to another prophecy, to another discerning of spirits, to another different kinds of tongues, to another the interpretation of tongues. But one and the same Spirit works all these things, distributing to each one individually as He wills.
—1 Corinthians 12:4-11

CATEGORY TWO: INSPIRATIONAL GIFTS

The second category is the speaking or inspirational gifts:

1. Different kinds of tongues
2. Interpreting tongues
3. Prophecy

Let's look at these three gifts and how they can operate in your life if the Holy Spirit blesses you with any of them.

Different Kinds of Tongues Gift

First, there is the gift of speaking in different kinds of tongues. Speaking in tongues is a supernatural utterance in an unknown tongue, inspired by the Holy Spirit. A person will speak in a language of the Spirit, a language that he or she has not known or learned previously. Most often, neither the speaker nor the listener will understand what is being said. The more you develop this gift, though, the more understanding will be available when you speak in tongues.

Speaking in different kinds of tongues is not the same as the baptism of the Holy Spirit. You get your own prayer language after you're baptized with the Holy Spirit. That's the evidence that you've been baptized. When you're filled with the Holy Spirit, you have the infilling, when the Holy Spirit convicts you and introduces Christ to your life. When you have the baptism of Holy Spirit you pray in your prayer language.

Interpretation of Tongues Gift

The second inspirational gift that follows the speaking of tongues is the interpretation of those different kinds of tongues. Usually, when there are diverse kinds of tongues in operation, somebody stands up and interprets the message being shared. This is how I know it's a genuine message in tongues. Mark 16:17 says, *"And these signs will follow those who believe: In My name they will cast out demons; they will speak with new tongues."*

Paul writes in First Corinthians 14:18, *"I thank my God I speak with tongues more than you all."* I believe, in this instance, he is talking about in his personal prayer language, which is what you receive after the baptism of the Holy Spirit. This is a precious and personal gift. Jude describes the benefit of praying in tongues in 1:20: *"But you, beloved, building yourselves up on your most holy faith, praying in the Holy Spirit."* But, this personal prayer language is distinct from both the gift of speaking in different tongues— previously unknown, world languages—and the interpretation of those languages for the edification of the Body.

The public ministry of tongues is a powerful gift to the community of believers. In First Corinthians 14:27-28, Paul writes, *"If anyone speaks in a tongue, let there be two or at the most three, each in turn, and let one interpret. But if there is no interpreter, let him keep silent in church, and let him speak to himself and to God."* Without an interpreter, speaking out in tongues in the midst of a church service could result in confusion. However, with an interpreter, an edifying message is able to be delivered to the Body.

Paul writes much about speaking in tongues. In First Corinthians 14:13-15 he writes:

Therefore let him who speaks in a tongue pray that he may interpret. For if I pray in a tongue, my spirit prays, but my understanding is unfruitful. What is the conclusion then? I will pray with the spirit, and I will also pray with the understanding. I will sing with the spirit, and I will also sing with the understanding.

Some people sing in tongues and then they give an interpretation. Some people speak in tongues and then somebody else interprets. Whatever the case may be, the purpose of both of these gifts is for the edification of believers. These two gifts combined— diverse kinds of tongues and the interpretation of tongues—are equal to the gift of prophecy.

If everyone who speaks in tongues goes into a Sunday service and stands up, speaking in Arabic while the pastor is delivering the message, nothing but confusion will be in the atmosphere. You must be sensitive to the Holy Spirit to know when the gifts are needed to operate in the service. God has a perfect time and for every gift to operate. The Bible says, *"Let all things be done decently and in order"* (1 Corinthians 14:40). These supernatural gifts are used by God to display His power through you as an individual.

Paul says in First Corinthians 14:5, *"I wish you all spoke with tongues, but even more that you prophesied; for he who prophesies is greater than he who speaks with tongues, unless indeed he interprets, that the church may receive edification."* Confusion had broken out in the Corinthian church, so apostle Paul clarifies their understanding of this gift. He had to explain how the gifts were supposed to operate, not because he wanted the Corinthians to stop, but because they needed further training.

To operate in either of these gifts takes a deeper level of faith, an even greater level than merely seeing and believing. Don't be afraid to step out there with a prophecy if God gave you something. Many people silence God speaking through them because they're afraid to get it wrong. Well, you're never going to know until you start opening your mouth. David wrote in Psalm 81:10, *"I am the Lord your God, who brought you out of the land of Egypt; open your mouth wide, and I will fill it."* So, open your mouth and He will fill it for His glory. God is waiting on you; the Holy Spirit is waiting on you.

Prophecy Gift

The third and final gift in the inspiration category is the gift of prophecy. What is the definition of prophecy? The definition is found in First Corinthians 14:1-5.

> **Pursue love, and desire spiritual gifts, but especially that you may prophesy.** For he who speaks in a tongue does not speak to men but to God, for no one understands him; however, in the spirit he speaks mysteries. But he who **prophesies speaks edification and exhortation and comfort** to men. He who speaks in a tongue edifies himself, but he **who prophesies edifies the church.** I wish you all spoke with tongues, but even more that you prophesied; for he **who prophesies is greater than he who speaks with tongues,** unless indeed he interprets, that the church may receive edification.

The gift of prophecy is a brief, supernatural utterance. True prophecy will never condemn or embarrass you. Additionally, prophecy—without a further word of knowledge—will not contain revelation. So, if you hear someone prophesy that the Lord said this or that is going to happen, that is not correct. The prophet Isaiah said, *"Thus says the Lord: 'Set your house in order, for you shall die, and not live.'"* When he spoke those words, he was operating in the office of a prophet, but he wasn't prophesying. In this moment, he was operating in the gifts of word of knowledge and word of wisdom. Do you see the difference?

The office of a prophet has all the revelation gifts and one of the power gifts. That's how you can tell the true ministry of a prophetess and prophet. Prophecy is an utterance by a believer that does not come from something a person already knows. In other words, let's say a person walks up to you and said, "I just got promoted. I've been waiting six months for it." Telling him that God has a new position for him is not a gift from God.

Don't be fooled by people who self-generate prophecies. Watch for those who wait until someone starts to cry before telling them that they're going through a hard time. It's obvious the person is having a rough time—there are tears. Sometimes someone will read people's emotions and then "prophesy." That's not the gifts of the Holy Spirit. When you have a real gift, you can see the brokenness without a single tear. There is nothing wrong with weeping in prayer, but a genuine gift of the Spirit doesn't rely on emotional cues from other in order to operate.

The misuse of the spiritual gifts has damaged many people. When someone believes the word of the prophet and then finds out it was a sham, they are understandably devastated. So, be careful when you operate and handle these gifts; cherish them, but realize that you're human and the Holy Spirit has to be the One to operate these gifts through you.

Remember, prophecy is a gift. It has nothing to do with your intellect, but everything to do with a supernatural revelation. Often this gift emerges when you or someone else is facing a critical or hard situation, and it looks too overwhelming to overcome. That is when the gifts begin to operate. You're dependent on a word from the Lord that will be meaningful to you. The purpose of the gift of prophecy is given in First Corinthians 14:3 New Living Translation: *"One who prophesies strengthens others, encourages them, and comforts them."* That is what the true gift for prophecy does.

Prophecy strengthens your inner self, lifting you up spiritually. Second, it is given to exhort, to urge. A special word may be given that will urge you or others to get closer to God, to obey Him, or to be strong in a crisis or temptation. Third, prophecy is for comfort in the age of tension and anxiety. In times of uncertainty, to receive a word from the Lord has a calming effect on our hearts.

Prophecy confirms more than it directs. It confirms a direction that God has already begun in your life. This is why it's important to understand that prophecy has to be confirmed on both ends of the line. If God spoke to somebody to give you a prophecy, nine times out of ten He's already talked to you about that same subject Himself or through one or more believers. The prophecy will just confirm His Word.

CATEGORY THREE: POWER GIFTS

The third category is power and the three gifts are:

1. Working of miracles
2. Faith
3. Gifts of healings

Working of Miracles

I get excited just hearing about the gift of working of miracles!

First of all, the gift of miracles will never make you an equal to Jesus; that's never going to happen. A miracle is a supernatural manifestation of God's power, of which humans and nature cannot explain its full meaning and purpose. Through working a miracle, people are given a glimpse of God's unlimited power. God intervenes and performs one of His works, and we call it a miracle. He simply calls it a work of the Father.

That's amazing to me. When I first began studying the gift of working in miracles many years ago, God began to teach me about these gifts. I marveled when I studied the operation of the gift of working miracles. I noticed that not only could Jesus operate in the gift of working in miracles as a man, but I realized that you and I can operate in the gifts of working of miracles too. We can have that same anointing, we can operate in that same faith, and we can go tap into the glory of God, witnessing the visible signs of His hands at work!

Miracles are encouraged by God. We are told in Scripture to ask Him for what we need (see Matt. 7:7). I remember in Orlando, Florida, there was a woman who was crippled. God gave me the word of knowledge about her, and the gift of working miracles began to operate. The woman had a walker, and when I moved the walker out of the way, the devil spoke to me, "So what are you going to do if God doesn't heal her?" And I said, "What are *you* going to do if God *does* heal her?"

All of a sudden God said, "Don't lay your hands on her." He called her by name, telling me the situation and her doctor's name. Immediately, the miracle began to manifest, and I could hear her bones popping. She stood up and started taking small steps. By the close of that revival, she was running around the room.

I'm excited to share this category of power gifts. Why? Because miracles are waiting to happen to you today. Every day you wake up, ask God for this gift to operate through you. Ask God to let miracles happen to you. There are miracles waiting with your name on them, defying all odds and all impossibilities. God specializes in the impossible. Luke 1:37, *"With God nothing is impossible."* And that same Holy Spirit is ready to do spiritual miracles through you.

Notice the definition of a gift of working miracles. Again, it's a supernatural work of God's power which cannot be fully explained by humans or natural law. This is not the gift of *creating* miracles, but the gift of *working* miracles. Why? God is the Creator, not you. You can see a created miracle, but it comes through the working of miracles gift from the Holy Spirit. When you see the working of miracles, it gives you an encounter with God's unlimited power. A miracle is an intervention in someone's life, performing the works of God. These are the works of our heavenly Father.

Jesus said that He did nothing that He didn't see His Father do (John 5:19). So, if you see Jesus doing it, then you can do it too. The Bible even tells us that Jesus said, *"Most assuredly, I say to you, he who believes in Me, the works that I do he will do also; and greater works than these he will do, because I go to My Father"* (John 14:12).

With the advanced in media and technology today, believers can have a platform that reaches the entire world. You can speak the Word of God over the airwaves, covering areas where you can't go physically and speaking God's miraculous power into people's lives. What a great treasure we have now to spread these gifts into a dying world that needs to see Jesus for the very first time. We are able to present the glory of God into realms that have never seen His power.

God uses human instruments to flow through for the working of His miracles. There are many examples in the Old Testament and the New Testament of His miraculous power manifest on the earth. Let's start with Elijah, the prophet and servant of God. Elijah confronts and challenges the prophets of Baal, the false god, in First Kings 18:20-40. They quickly realized that God Almighty was the one true God when:

> *The fire of the Lord fell and consumed the burnt sacrifice, and the wood and the stones and the dust, and it licked up the water that was in the trench. Now when all the people saw it, they fell on their faces; and they said, "The Lord, He is God! The Lord, He is God!"*

No idols or image can measure up to the authority of the Almighty God. And God's power is woven throughout the Bible.

There are so many examples, in the life of Christ, of the working of miracles in the New Testament. It's said that Christ worked about thirty-three recorded miracles during His ministry, including:

- Changing water into wine, John 2:9
- Healing the lame man, John 5:5-8
- Walking on water, Matthew 14:22-33
- Healing two blind men, Matthew 9:27-30
- Feeding thousands with five loaves of bread and two fish, Matthew 14:13-21
- Restoring life to Lazarus, His friend, John 11:43-44
- Reattaching a servant's ear, Luke 22:49-51

What awesome miracles! There are many more examples of the gift of working miracles, but these few provide evidence of this gift of the Holy Spirit operating throughout the New and Old Testaments. This gift is waiting for you—grasp every opportunity. If you have the desire to see miracles, start seeking this gift and you'll be amazed what God can do through you.

Gift of Faith

The next gift within the power category is the gift of faith. The gift of faith is a deeper form of your day-to-day faith. This deeper faith usually comes to you when you have a critical need, or your heart is filled with confusion or uncertainty. This gift, like every other spiritual gift, operates as the Holy Spirit wills, not as you will. The gift of faith is given when there is doubt or the spirit of fear. I've seen this gift operate more than I have the other gifts. It brings a supernatural faith when, filled with fear or double, you're facing a situation that looks impossible.

I call it "God's kind of faith"—an extraordinary faith. Jesus spoke to the natural elements of the world and, when His disciples were overcome with fear, He commanded the waves and the winds to be still. That was the gift of faith in operation.

We can see the distinction between saving faith and general faith in the Bible. In Ephesians 2:8, it says, *"For by grace you have been saved through faith, and that not of yourselves; it is the gift of God."* Every believer has some measure of general faith, as Paul tells us in Romans 12:3. The fruit of faith or faithfulness from the Holy Spirit revealed in Galatians 5:22-23. The gift of faith, though, is a supernatural gift that the Holy Spirit chooses to impart to a believer. With this gift, a positive knowing without any question is released to the particular believer.

> *Now faith is the substance of things hoped for, the evidence of things not seen. ...By faith we understand that the worlds were framed by the word of God, so that the things which are seen were not made of things which are visible* (Hebrews 11:1,3).

When you see the gift of faith operate, there are no questions or doubts. It settles every matter of the heart and every issue, including faith for healing.

> *But Jesus turned around, and when He saw her He said, "Be of good cheer, daughter; your faith has made you well." And the woman was made well from that hour* (Matthew 9:22).

Then Jesus said to him, "Go your way; your faith has
made you well." And immediately he received his sight
and followed Jesus on the road (Mark 10:52).

Gifts of Healings

The last gift in the power category is the gifts of healings.
It's the only gift that the apostle Paul uses in a plural context.
Individuals may be given the gift for a specific area of the physical
body. For instance, someone may have the gift of healing for a person's damaged back. Every time this gifted person lays hands on
someone's back, the person is immediately healed. Someone else
may have the gift of healings for blind eyes.

Whatever the area is that God begins to reveal to you, that's
how the gifts of healings will work through you. It is impossible for
the gifts of healing to operate through you without compassion.
So, if you don't have a desire to see the sick healed or you are both-
ered by seeing people suffering, you may not be used by the Holy
Spirit with this gifting.

I remember when I first received this gift, I was in a place of
seeking God. Every time I saw someone with a disease or handi-
cap, I would weep with compassion. I had a hatred toward disease.
I hate the devil and I know the feeling is mutual. When I see
people with sickness and disease, it does something inside me. It
makes me want to fast more and do whatever I have to do to help
that person receive a miracle.

*And **Jesus** went about all Galilee, teaching in their*
synagogues, preaching the gospel of the kingdom, and

> **healing all kinds of sickness and all kinds of disease** *among the people* (Matthew 4:23).

If your heart is stirred with compassion for those who are ill and hurting, maybe you need to seek the gifts of healings. Not everybody has that desire. Jesus knew He had the gifts of healings and He healed multitudes during His ministry. He was so compassionate that He actually felt the healing virtue leaving His body. Jesus, immediately knowing in Himself that power had gone out of Him, turned around in the crowd and said:

> *"Who touched My clothes?" But His disciples said to Him, "You see the multitude thronging You, and You say, 'Who touched Me?'" And He looked around to see her who had done this thing. But the woman, fearing and trembling, knowing what had happened to her, came and fell down before Him and told Him the whole truth. And He said to her, "Daughter, your faith has made you well. Go in peace, and be healed of your affliction"* (Mark 5:30-35).

Healing had gone out of Him from the Holy Spirit through the gifts of healings.

> *And **Jesus** went about all Galilee, teaching in their synagogues, preaching the gospel of the kingdom, and **healing all kinds of sickness and all kinds of disease** among the people* (Matthew 4:23).

Another example of Jesus' compassion and gift comes from Matthew 8:1-3:

When He had come down from the mountain, great multitudes followed Him. And behold, a leper came and worshiped Him, saying, "Lord, if You are willing, You can make me clean." Then Jesus put out His hand and touched him, saying, "I am willing; be cleansed." Immediately his leprosy was cleansed.

I've heard this conversation for years throughout the healing ministry: Is it God's will for me to be healed? Yes, it is God's will. Well, if it's God's will, why isn't everybody healed? I've learned that there are some things humans will never know about healing on this side of Heaven. But I *do* know, without a shadow of a doubt, it is God's will for you to be healed. When you continue to trust in faith in the Lord Jesus Christ, God will manifest a miracle for you.

I encourage you to go after the heart of the Holy Spirit, seek Him for His gifts, and then watch God give you one of those nine gifts to operate through you. Then, you can encourage someone who needs to be encouraged, healed, lifted up in faith, receive wisdom and knowledge, or receive their prayer language. May you be a willing vessel for God.

I want to pray over you:

Father, in the name of Jesus, I pray now that You will touch this reader with Your love and wisdom. Let the gifts of the Spirit be in operation. Touch and encourage this person as only You can. I command the powers of darkness to be broken, every form of witchcraft to be broken. I release the Holy Spirit and

His gifts to be imparted to your life, that you may see the greater glory manifest on you and come into your life. May you be a voice in the earth, speaking, encouraging people on the pathway to victory. Amen.

God bless you.

PRAYER OF IMPARTATION

Heavenly Father, I ask that you will open the Heavens and pour out Your Spirit upon this child of Yours reading this book. May the Gifts of the Holy Spirit begin to manifest in their life and may they see many miracles, signs, and wonders wrought through their hands as You use them in these gifts. May the glory of Heaven rest upon their lives continually and may they enter into a deeper relationship with You. In Jesus' name I pray, amen.

But the manifestation of the Spirit is given to every man to profit withal (1 Corinthians 12:7 KJV).

7 | UNLOCKING GLORY IN YOUR LIFE

*H*ow do you unlock supernatural glory in your life? The key is simple: serve others. The gift of serving unlocks supernatural activity into every area of your life. When we examine the lives of two great men of God—Elijah the prophet and, Elisha, his student—we can see this truth manifest.

When we think of the ministry of Elijah, what often comes to mind is all of the opposition he endured and overcame throughout his ministry. For example, the false prophets of Jezebel—a wicked goddess—were no match for Elijah's faith in God. When we study Elijah's ministry, we can come to understand the boldness he imparted into the life of Elisha.

On their journey together, Elijah first took Elisha to Gilgal. The meaning of Gilgal is "turning point." Elisha was a young prophet with stars in his eyes. He thought he understood all there was to know about the ministry of the prophet and about receiving Elijah's mantle. He thought he knew how he was going to be promoted into the role of Elijah as a great prophet, but Elijah had something to teach his young student about obeying God. So, they went to Gilgal—the turning point.

Before Elijah was supernaturally taken up to Heaven in a whirlwind, he faced many challenges. And, through them all, Elisha stayed by his side. Let's follow along in the Bible's story as told in Second Kings:

> And it came to pass, when the Lord was about to take up Elijah into heaven by a whirlwind, that Elijah went with Elisha from Gilgal. Then Elijah said to Elisha, "Stay here, please, for the Lord has sent me on to Bethel."
>
> But Elisha said, "As the Lord lives, and as your soul lives, I will not leave you!" So they went down to Bethel.
>
> Now the sons of the prophets who were at Bethel came out to Elisha, and said to him, "Do you know that the Lord will take away your master from over you today?"
>
> And he said, "Yes, I know; keep silent!"
>
> Then Elijah said to him, "Elisha, stay here, please, for the Lord has sent me on to Jericho."

But he said, "As the Lord lives, and as your soul lives, I will not leave you!" So they came to Jericho.

Now the sons of the prophets who were at Jericho came to Elisha and said to him, "Do you know that the Lord will take away your master from over you today?"

So he answered, "Yes, I know; keep silent!"

Then Elijah said to him, "Stay here, please, for the Lord has sent me on to the Jordan."

But he said, "As the Lord lives, and as your soul lives, I will not leave you!" So the two of them went on. And fifty men of the sons of the prophets went and stood facing them at a distance, while the two of them stood by the Jordan. Now Elijah took his mantle, rolled it up, and struck the water; and it was divided this way and that, so that the two of them crossed over on dry ground.

And so it was, when they had crossed over, that Elijah said to Elisha, "Ask! What may I do for you, before I am taken away from you?"

Elisha said, "Please let a double portion of your spirit be upon me" (2 Kings 2:1-9).

Elisha was faced with a decision. He had to make up his mind about going with Elijah or staying back as he told him to do. He had to choose between what Elijah was telling him to do and what Elisha believed God had assigned to him.

There comes a moment in every believer's life when—like Elisha—they have to decide whether they will seek God and obey His instructions or not. Elijah wanted to know how hungry Elisha was for God's glory. How hungry are *you* for the anointing? Will you disregard and disobey God? Your decision will set you on a course that will either result in abundance or darkness.

You have a call on your life. The gifts to enable the fulfillment of this call have been assigned to you. And you have to come to a moment when you decide. Am I going to obey the Lord or am I going to listen to the enemy? Whatever God asks of you, do it with the most respect, humility, and honor.

The Four Stages of Entering the Glory Realm

Stage One: Faith

Elijah told Elisha to stay in Gilgal—the turning point—while he went on to Bethel. Elisha had a decision to make. When you are faced with a decision, don't contemplate or second guess what God wants you to do. Step out on the realms of faith and believe God. Faith causes miracles. Faith is a magnetic force that bring miracles to you, but you have to step out into the realm of faith. When you see faith moving, move with it.

God is waiting for you to obey His voice. At the turning point, Elisha learned to follow in the footsteps of the prophet of God, Elijah, and to serve him. What you make happen for others, God will make happen for you. Many times, your miracle comes when you are helping someone else. Many times, when you pray for somebody, your prayer is also heard. When you help someone else, God helps you.

Stage Two: Persistence

The second place Elijah taught Elisha was Bethel, meaning the House of God or the House of Bread. This is where Elisha learned about revelation. During the second stage of entering the glory realm, Elisha learned how to be persistent and determined. People tried to discourage him from staying with Elijah, reminding him that Elijah would soon be taken away.

If you have a mentor who is aligned with God's Word and you serve that person, that person's gift can come onto you if the Holy Spirit allows it. Your mentor's gift unlocks the heavenly realms and the supernatural gift in you. So, keep serving and do it unto the Lord. Matthew 6 is loaded with godly principles for this kind of service. Whatever you do, do it unto the Lord secretly, and He will reward you openly.

Elijah and Elisha went to Bethel—the House of God, the place of vision, and the place of bread. The House of God is where you're taught the Word of God. The Bible tells us about the value of going to church in Hebrews: *"not forsaking the assembling of ourselves together"* (Hebrews 10:25). We need our faith to be encouraged. We need our spirits to be encouraged. And the House of God is where that happens. When you hear a testimony from someone who was blessed by the Lord, it builds your faith. When you are settled in a house of God, you become rooted, stable, unable to be tossed about by present circumstances.

So, the second stage to unlocking the supernatural that Elisha discovered is being persistent in finding a house of God where you can be taught the Word of God. There, you can discover Him more deeply, developing your understanding until you are sent out. Whatever assignment is on your life, God will reveal it to you, oftentimes through a leader, pastor, or mentor. Gifts are assigned to every believer on planet Earth. And God is waiting for you to get established in a House of God, learn His Word, and grow in the things of the Lord Jesus Christ by meditating on His Word day and night.

Bethel can also be understood as the intimate place of connection with God, like your prayer closet. This second stage is all about seeking God and dedicating yourself to Him like Elisha did to Elijah. Invest yourself in the realm of prayer. Get in conversation with God. Tell him, as Elisha told Elijah, "I will not leave You, Lord. As long as my body lives here on earth, I will not leave You. As long as I'm still alive, I will not leave Your side. I'm not going to take my eyes off You. I desire only You, Lord. I want You in my life always." If your desire is for God's anointing, you can tap into His glory with persistent commitment.

When you pursue the anointing with all your heart, you will go through these first two stages: in Gilgal you will make up your mind not to listen to the lies of the devil or think about your past mistakes. And, then, you will declare at Bethel, "I'm going to go for it. I'm going to attend a house of God where I will be rooted and grounded in the things of God. I'm going to be taught. I'm going to be developed so I can grow in character with integrity so when somebody sees my life, they will see a reflection of God."

You have to be determined and persistent as never before. If you really want God's blessing and anointing, you will hunger and thirst after it. David said, *"As the deer pants for the water brooks, so pants my soul for You, O God. My soul thirsts for God, for the living God…"* (Psalm 42:1-2). You have to have a thirst and a hunger. I tell evangelists and pastors, "If you want a real move of God, you have to have an appetite for it." The glory will never manifest if you don't have an appetite for the glory. If you have an appetite for the glory, I promise you, God will come down in the form of a pillar of fire or a cloud by day. Some way or another, God's going to reveal who He is, His nature, and His purpose in your life.

Stage Three: Warfare

When Elijah and Elisha traveled to Jericho, Elisha learned a crucial lesson about the third stage of entering the glory realm: spiritual warfare. He had to learn strategies for facing and overcoming demonic powers. Spiritual warfare comes in all shapes and sizes, but protecting your spiritual atmosphere is of the utmost importance.

The company you keep influences your spiritual atmosphere greatly, helping to determine the outcome of your destiny. Because of this, it is very important to be intentional with who you are surrounding yourself with and who you allow to speak into your life. Joseph learned this the hard way when he acted outside of God's timing and shared his dream with his brothers. He allowed their doubt to influence him, and this caused him to go through many trials that he could have otherwise avoided. In other words, only allow righteous, godly people to become close friends and/or associates. Do they have your same spiritual outlook? Do they respect your heart? Can you share your dreams with them?

Elisha had a lesson to learn about maintaining his own spiritual atmosphere through spiritual warfare. Elijah instructed Elisha, explaining about the spirit realm in a way that may have sounded something like, "I know you're young and you want to learn about God and you're eager and you're excited—but beyond your excitement, the anointing is so precious that it can bless your life or it can destroy your life. You can walk prematurely, and it can destroy your life. You can get ahead of God's timing and you can abort your destiny. You can get spiritual burnout and throw your hands up." Elisha was going to have to learn about spiritual warfare on the road to Jericho if he was going to sustain the call on his life.

When most believers think about Jericho, Joshua and Israel's army marching around the walls of Jericho comes to mind (see Joshua 6). The significance of this story is that the Lord gave Joshua a strategy that taught him and the people of Israel how to be still. There are times when you don't need to say anything, just follow God's instructions. So many times, we want to speak out when what we really need to say is nothing; be silent and let God fight the battle instead of fighting it ourselves.

> Joshua had commanded the people, saying, "You shall not shout or make any noise with your voice, nor shall a word proceed out of your mouth, until the day I say to you, 'Shout!' Then you shall shout" (Joshua 6:10).

Learning to be victorious in spiritual warfare is the third stage. Jericho and its impenetrable walls represent warfare. You can tell the level of the anointing on a person's life by the warfare that the person has experienced. Often, though, it's not obvious because the battles they faced happened in private—between the enemy and the Spirit-filled person. In other words, when you look at a person's ministry, life, and the anointing that he or she carries, ask yourself what this person may have gone through that you don't know about. My mentor Brother Schambach told me, "In order to walk in our footsteps, what are you willing to go through?"

Many are quick to want a double portion of someone else's anointing without knowing that they are also asking for double warfare. Are you willing to go through double the trouble? The anointing will cost you everything. That is what Elijah was trying to explain to Elisha. In essence, he was telling his young student, "I know you're excited now, but there's going to come a time when you're not going to be excited. You're going to face witches. You're going to face warfare. You're going to face demonic powers. You're going to see demonic strongholds. You're going to feel like satan is snapping at your heels. When all hell is coming against you, can you remain standing to be blessed?"

I'll never forgot a private moment in one of the biggest ministries I've served. After a successful meeting, packed with people, I was in a back room and saw one of my mentors crying like a baby. I said, "Man, you just got to minister to thousands of people...miracles happened." His response has stayed with my all the years. He said, "Tracy, never get caught up in the crowds. Stay *with* the crowd. I wonder how many thousands really got ahold of the message. Maybe between one and five people out of thousands truly caught the revelation of the glory of God." Then, he said, "Tracy, what the churches want now is entertainment. But what God is looking for are true vessels He can operate His glory through in order to manifest His purpose."

So, don't be discouraged when you see warfare break out. Nobody wants to go through warfare, but it comes along with the anointing. It squeezes you. But the more God squeezes you, the more of the old flows out and away and the His anointing fills you. Warfare is an indication that you have a promotion within reach. In other words, your past victories are signs that you have not only survived, but you're ready for revival.

The army of Joshua marched around the walls of Jericho silently, according to God's command. But, when Joshua gave the order to shout, the walls—the strongholds—came tumbling down! God's instructions contain strategy to overcome the opposition and experience victory. Even Jesus knew that God's will was the only way to fulfill His mandate on the earth. And, Jesus knew that God's anointing and gifts followed from serving. *"Just as the Son of Man did not come to be served, but to serve, and to give His life a ransom for many"* (Matthew 20:28). The key to accessing spiritual glory in your life is to serve others—like Christ—with compassion and dedication. When you serve as Jesus Christ served, you will experience success as well as warfare. You will have to fight like never before.

When you go through spiritual warfare, remember that you've been prepared by the Holy Spirit. Nothing will take you off-guard unless you are not seeking the Lord and not praying. If you pray and seek God daily, I promise you, He'll show you the snares and traps of the enemy. And even when you do fall into an enemy's trap, you can get back on your feet, tell the devil he's a liar, and claim victory in the name of Jesus.

The walls of Jericho tumbled down because Joshua listened for and obeyed the Lord. What walls do you have in your life that you want to tumble down and be destroyed? They will fall when you begin obeying God and serving others. The walls may be financial trouble, family matters, children, your job, whatever the case may be you can overcome each one. Anytime you experience opposition, it's an indication that a breakthrough is within reach. Whenever you see the devil causing chaos, go ahead and give God praise because He's getting ready to give you a breakthrough. God wants to calm the troubles waters in your soul. Serving unlocks the supernatural glory in your personal life and reveals keys for you to tap into the glory of God.

Stage Four: Deliverance and Double Portion

> Then Elijah said to him [Elisha], "Stay here, please, for the Lord has sent me on to the Jordan." But he said, "**As the Lord lives, and as your soul lives, I will not leave you!**" So the two of them went on. And fifty men of the sons of the prophets went and stood facing them at a distance, while the two of them stood by the Jordan. Now Elijah took his mantle, rolled it up, and struck the water; and it was divided this way and that, so that the two of them crossed over on dry ground. And so it was, when they had crossed over, that Elijah said to Elisha, "Ask! What may I do for you, before I am taken away from you?" Elisha said, "Please let a **double portion of your spirit** be upon me" (2 Kings 2:6-9).

Elijah told Elisha to remain where he was while he went on to the River Jordan, testing his commitment again. Elisha confirmed that he would not leave Elijah—he would travel with him again, this time to Jordan. First, Elijah delivered them from harm by using his mantle—his anointing—to cause the water to part so they could cross the river. Then, Elisha told his mentor that he would like a double portion of his anointing. At this fourth and final stage of entering the glory realm, we need to reconfirm our commitment to our Father in Heaven. In turn, He will deliver us and give us a double portion of the anointing to empower the life He designed for each of us.

Not only did Elijah and Elisha have a life-changing moment at the Jordan River, that same river is also where Jesus, John the Baptist, and the Holy Spirit had a powerful encounter:

> It came to pass in those days that Jesus came from Nazareth of Galilee, and was baptized by John in the Jordan. And immediately, coming up from the water, He saw the heavens parting and the Spirit descending upon Him like a dove. Then a voice came from heaven, "You are My beloved Son, in whom I am well pleased" (Mark 1:7-8).

Jesus lifted up His eyes after being baptized in the Jordan, and the Holy Spirit came upon Him in the form of a dove. God was saying in essence, "My Son is going to carry out the hardest task. He's going to be crucified. He's going to be rejected even by His own people. He's going to go to the Garden of Gethsemane, and then to the Cross on Calvary to save humankind from themselves. To redeem them one by one."

*The next day John saw Jesus coming toward him, and said, "**Behold! The Lamb of God who takes away the sin of the world!** This is He of whom I said, 'After me comes a Man who is preferred before me, for He was before me.' I did not know Him; but that He should be revealed to Israel, therefore I came baptizing with water." And John bore witness, saying, "**I saw the Spirit descending from heaven like a dove, and He remained upon Him.** I did not know Him, but He who sent me to baptize with water said to me, 'Upon whom you see the Spirit descending, and remaining on Him, **this is He who baptizes with the Holy Spirit.**' And I have seen and testified that **this is the Son of God.**" (John 1:29-34).*

This is a powerful statement. God already knows your end before you even start, just like He knew His Son was going to become the supreme Sacrifice for all humankind so that our sins would be forgiven. He said, "This is My beloved Son in whom I am well pleased." He was already pleased with Jesus before He ever rode into Jerusalem with shouts of Hosanna, before He performed any miracles, before He even went to Gethsemane and was crucified.

Going to Jordan—the place of deliverance—reminds me of Elisha and Naaman, who had leprosy.

Now Naaman, commander of the army of the king of Syria, was a great and honorable man in the eyes of his master, because by him the Lord had given victory to Syria. He was also a mighty man of valor, but a leper. And the Syrians had gone out on raids, and had brought back captive a young girl from the land of Israel. She waited on Naaman's wife. Then she said to her mistress, "If only my master were with the prophet who is in Samaria! For he would heal him of his leprosy." ...Then Naaman went with his horses and chariot, and he stood at the door of Elisha's house. And Elisha sent a messenger to him, saying, "Go and wash in the Jordan seven times, and your flesh shall be restored to you, and you shall be clean." But Naaman became furious, and went away and said, "Indeed, I said to myself, 'He will surely come out to me, and stand and call on the name of the Lord his God, and wave his hand over the place, and heal the leprosy.' Are not the Abanah and the Pharpar, the rivers of Damascus, better than all the waters of Israel? Could I not wash in them and be clean?" So he turned and went away in a rage. And his servants came near and spoke to him, and said, "My father, if the prophet had told you to do something great, would you not have done it? How much more then, when he says to you, 'Wash, and be clean'?" So he went down and dipped seven times in the Jordan, according to the saying of the man of God; and his flesh was restored like the flesh of a little child, and he was clean (2 Kings 5:1-14).

When we, in our arrogance, take our eyes off God and think we know better, we will not be healed. Our job is to be a person

God can use to serve and help others and to thank Him for whom-ever He uses to help us. God is the one who does the miracles, not us. If we are experiencing the supernatural, we need to remember that God is flowing through us. We can be replaced, but He can't. The moment we think we cannot be replaced is the moment we have stepped into pride and arrogance. The greater the platform we have, the more important it is for us to remain humble. The Bible says the greatest servant among you all shall be the servant of all (see Matthew 23:11). If Jesus washed His disciples' feet, how much more shall we stay humble?

Elisha was at the final stage of tapping into the glory realm and seeing a double portion anointing manifest on his life. But, before Elijah was taken up to Heaven in the whirlwind, Elisha had to be delivered of anything and everything that might have held him back from being the servant of God he needs to be to receive the anointing. This is true for all of us. Before we can receive the double portion of anointing, we have to be delivered.

Elisha had proceeded through the first three stages: he had faith in God that his mentor would lead him toward the greater realm of glory; he was determined and persistent to stay the course; he claimed victory over spiritual warfare; and now he would experience deliverance and be given a double portion of anointing.

All along, Elijah was teaching the young prophet—about the gifts, the battles, the miracles—and Elisha was accumulating testimonies of God's power every step of the way. Now, he needed to be delivered. Elijah used his mantle to part the Jordan River so they could leave behind the past and step into the new. Likewise, you need to be set free from any unrighteous ways, manners, and/

or habits. When you walk through the waters that God parts with gratitude and humility, you will replace the garment of heaviness and put on the garment of praise.

Elijah led the way for Elisha, acting as his spiritual mentor. God places people around us who will help us steward our destinies. These mentors will encourage us, help us, and push us into receiving our breakthroughs. The mentors, like Elijah, often recognize both the call on our lives as well as God's timing for us even better than we can on our own. Understanding what season, we're in is crucial to sustaining God's will for our lives. We need to be aware of God's perfect timing.

> And so it was, when they had crossed over, that Elijah said to Elisha, "**Ask!** What may I do for you, before I am taken away from you?" Elisha said, "**Please let a double portion of your spirit be upon me.**" So he said, "**You have asked a hard thing. Nevertheless, if you see me when I am taken from you, it shall be so for you**; but if not, it shall not be so." Then it happened, as they continued on and talked, that **suddenly a chariot of fire appeared** with horses of fire, and separated the two of them; **and Elijah went up by a whirlwind into heaven.** And Elisha saw it, and he cried out, "My father, my father, the chariot of Israel and its horsemen!" So he saw him no more. And he took hold of his own clothes and tore them into two pieces. **He also took up the mantle of Elijah that had fallen from him,** and went back and stood by the bank of the Jordan (2 Kings 2:9-13).

Elijah discovered the final key—his servanthood was rewarded. He may have thought, *All that I've dedicated my time, my effort, my resources, I'm finally going to see the rewards.* I want to encourage you, dear reader, that, like Elisha, your sowing and serving is not in vain. Your tithing, your giving, whatever you have done to promote someone else's vision—your work was not in vain. The rewards are going to be greater than your trials or the time that you gave. When you continue in the service of the Lord Jesus Christ, you're going to receive His glory.

The apostle Paul said to his mentee, Timothy:

> *I have fought the good fight, I have finished the race, I have kept the faith. Finally, there is laid up for me the crown of righteousness, which the Lord, the righteous Judge, will give to me on that Day, and not to me only but also to all who have loved His appearing* (2 Timothy 4:7-10).

When we have fought that last battle, God will show us the ultimate glory realm. He will take home all who obeyed Him, believed in Him, spread His Gospel, and walked in His ways.

Elisha stayed with Elijah until *"he saw him no more"* (2 Kings 2:12). The whirlwind had separated them. He saw the miraculous, but didn't get distracted from God's call on his life. Elisha picked up Elijah's mantle from the ground and, with it, served the Lord with a double portion of anointing. The greatest lesson Elijah taught Elisha was to keep his eyes on God—not Elijah or even on himself.

Second Kings 2:14 reveals the secret to the heavenly key to access, to unlock the spiritual gifts from the heavenly realm:

> *Then he took the mantle of Elijah that had fallen from him, and struck the water, and said,* **"Where is the Lord God of Elijah?"** *And when he also had struck the water, it was divided this way and that; and Elisha crossed over.*

That's the key—he's not only the God of Elijah, He's not only Deborah's God, He's not only Abraham's God or Esther's God. He's your God too! Are you going to pick up the mantle, the anointing God has for you? There's a mission that He's called you to accomplish. In obedience and commitment, God will show you what He wants you to do. You may receive a dream or vision, or prophetic word—however He reveals to you, follow through. Go to Jordan, use the keys you've gathered and unlock the supernatural gifts for God's glory. Use these gifts to serve the people around you at work, school, or wherever there is a need. The heavenly gifts are ready to operate in your life as an individual and as a believer in His Church—you will be amazed at what God does through you.

The glory is waiting for an invitation of obedience from you. When you obey God, you automatically open the door of glory. Follow the footsteps that God ordained for you. Serve. And remember, there will be times when others have the spotlight on them and their gifts shine. Your gifts may be in the background, but don't feel overlooked. God sees everything you do for Him. Keep serving, because your serving will promote you and put you on platforms that will make you marvel. You'll think, *How in the world did I get here?* You're going to be amazed at the things God does through you.

I'm going to pray that a double portion of God's anointing will come on your life:

> *Father, in the name of Jesus, we saw through the lives of Elijah and Elisha that Elisha received a double portion of Your anointing because he had faith, was persistent, fought the good fight, and was delivered. I pray that this reader will follow their footsteps as You lead. I pray that Your glory would surround and overwhelm this person today and every day. Now, it's time that you make up your mind, get in the house of God, and be obedient to the ways of the Lord. You can have power over the devil. You don't have to be intimidated by demonic powers. Be victorious in spiritual warfare. And remember, friend, anytime spiritual warfare breaks out, it's just a sign there's a breakthrough within reach. So, don't get discouraged, the angels are moving on your behalf.*
>
> *Go to Jordan; you can find deliverance. Whatever you've been going through up to this moment, God's going to release double blessings for your trouble. I release the anointing on your life. I release the gifts into your life. Be blessed and know that God hears you and will answer you in Jesus' mighty name. Amen.*

God bless you.

PRAYER OF IMPARTATION

Father, in Jesus' name, I pray that through the glory of God you will make yourself known that they will come to a revelation of who the Holy Spirit is and His gifts in their lives. As they carry the glory of God that Your purpose will be made known and that they will pursue it. In Jesus' name, amen.

And the glory of the Lord shall be revealed, and all flesh shall see it together: for the mouth of the Lord hath spoken it (Isaiah 40:5 KJV).

8 | THE TIME OF VISITATION

*E*veryone has a calling and gifts assigned to their lives. But we need heavenly keys to unlock and access our supernatural, spiritual gifts. We have to discover the revelation of what that assignment is so we can fulfill God's plan—for us and His Kingdom. Now, we need to look at the time of visitation—the importance of positioning yourself in the spirit of submission for the glory.

Acts 7:45-55 tells us of the priests' reaction to Stephen the martyr's dedication to sharing the truth of the Gospel and shedding light on how Israel rebelled against God:

> *When they heard these things they were cut to the heart, and they gnashed at him with their teeth. But*

> *he, being full of the Holy Spirit, looked steadfastly into heaven, and saw the glory of God, and Jesus standing on the right hand of God. He saw the heavens open, and the Son of man standing on the right hand of God.*

This is the first time in Scripture that we read of Jesus *standing* on the right hand of God. He was recognizing Stephen's bold statements and was so touched with the sacrifice of His servant that he took notice of it; it became a sweet fragrance.

> *Then they cried out with a loud voice, stopped their ears, and ran at him [Stephen] with one accord; and they cast him out of the city and stoned him. ...they stoned Stephen as he was calling on God and saying, "Lord Jesus, receive my spirit." Then he knelt down and cried out with a loud voice, "Lord, do not charge them with this sin." And when he had said this, he fell asleep.*

Are you ready to position yourself for the same glory that this man of God, Stephen, who was stoned to death? I'm not necessarily talking about being martyred for God, but there are levels of persecution that often come against us. And we need to each examine our hearts to see how determined we are to continue giving our lives to the Lord, when trials come, so He can fulfill His purpose.

THE TIME OF VISITATION

We must each position ourselves to receive a visitation of the glory. In other words, we need to be in a place where we can be on the receiving end of all that God wants us to have so that we are able to fulfill our purpose here on earth.

> *For days will come upon you when your enemies will build an embankment around you, surround you and close you in on every side, and level you, and your children within you, to the ground; and they will not leave in you one stone upon another, because you did not know the time of your visitation* (Luke 19:43-44).

We must first know when to anticipate a visitation of the glory. How do you know when it's time? You've been praying. You've been fasting. You've been giving and serving. Now, it's time for God to come to you and reveal His plans for your life. Jeremiah 29:11, *"'I know the thoughts that I think toward you,' says the Lord, 'thoughts of peace and not of evil, to give you a future and a hope.'"*

Are you ready for God to visit you? Are you ready to hear God's voice? Are you ready to know God more deeply than you have ever known Him? Are you ready to go where you've never gone? Are you ready to challenge your old mind-sets? Are you ready to go to that next step where God can encourage you as Elijah encouraged and taught Elisha?

When we've done all that we know to do, it's in God's hands to bless us. And He wants to put His glory on us so we can be glory carriers on earth. Luke 19:43-44 tells us that, sadly, many people miss their time of visitation because they are distracted. There were five wise virgins who were prepared for their bridegroom and five foolish virgins who were not. The five foolish women carried on with their everyday lives so, when their bridegroom called for them, they had no oil in their lamps—their lights went out. The excitement of life—the anointing—was gone from their lives.

The five wise virgins, on the other hand, kept oil burning in their lamps. God wants to keep the oil of the Holy Spirit fresh, burning in you just like He did with David. Samuel anointed David with oil, which is why he could slay the giant, Goliath. David was anointed to be a shepherd over Israel, overcoming both the bear and the lion. David knew that God would help him overcome every obstacle.

Like it did with David, anointing oil sets you up for fulfilling a special purpose. When the oil begins to flow through you, you will feel it in your hands, your feet. All of a sudden you move into a place of dancing and praising the Lord. You will be able to feel His anointing, because God is bearing witness that He's with you and He's upon you. When it's time for a visitation of the glory, welcome that season. Don't miss the opportunity that's knocking at the doors of your heart.

Let's read an important and interesting passage from the Song of Solomon:

> *I slept, but my heart was awake, when I heard my lover knocking and calling: "Open to me, my treasure, my darling, my dove, my perfect one. My head is drenched with dew, my hair with the dampness of the night."*
>
> *But I responded, "I have taken off my robe. Should I get dressed again? I have washed my feet. Should I get them soiled?"*

My lover tried to unlatch the door, and my heart thrilled within me. I jumped up to open the door for my love, and my hands dripped with perfume. My fingers dripped with lovely myrrh as I pulled back the bolt.

I opened to my lover, but he was gone! My heart sank. I searched for him but could not find him anywhere. I called to him, but there was no reply (Song of Solomon 5:2-6 NLT).

You can sense the disheartened one who missed the visitation in these verses. Don't miss your time of visitation. Whatever you have to do to fit private time with God into your day—do it. Get serious with God. Fall on your knees. Call upon the Lord while He is near. Seek Him. Ask of Him and you shall receive.

You need to know the time of visitation is an open opportunity for you to begin your assignment. Put aside excuses and respond sincerely. Put aside every sin that so easily distracts you; run the race that's set before you, for the race is not given to the swift nor the strong, but to the one who endures until the end (Hebrews 12:1; 1 Corinthians 9:24). Continue marching on and pursuing with the strength of the Holy Spirit to fulfill the Great Commission.

There are times when it seems the heavens are like iron and you can't penetrate that ceiling with your prayers—no matter how many prayers you pray. But there are also times when the heavens are open and your prayers are heard and answered immediately. When you're operating under an open heaven, healing and miracles take place, prayers are answered, and you will see His glory shining through.

Our world needs a time of visitation. Our churches, our family, our personal life, all need God's glory, and we can position ourselves to receive it. I want you to know that God is sending His angels down from Heaven through the portals of glory, looking throughout the earth to find those whom He can use to advance His Kingdom. Remember, God has to display His glory through humans just like He did through Moses, David, Esther, and thousands of others throughout the Bible. God is ready to channel His presence, His glory, and His anointing through you!

Do not miss your visitation—get to know God in such a way that He becomes your Beloved. Seek a deep and personal relationship with Him. He knows you personally, and He wants you to know Him personally. He's your Friend. You're not just a disciple to Him, you're His close confident.

God will share His secrets and His heart with you when you become His friend. He will let you know what's troubling Him. Then, you can help Him minister to the needs of the broken, battered, or bruised people in your corner of the world. We have to put aside our excuses and respond to the Holy Spirit's conviction and to His causes.

Angelic Visits

When your time of visitation arrives and the heavens are open, angels begin to visit you and minister to you. Hebrews 1:14 says that angels are ministering spirits sent forth to minister to those who will inherit salvation. Throughout the Old and New Testaments, angels of God come to the rescue of many people. Jacob saw angels of God ascending and descending on a ladder. He saw the moment of visitation and grabbed ahold of it, literally.

During the scuffle with the angel, his hip fell out of joint. Walking from that moment on with a limp, he learned to be dependent on the Lord and His timing rather than himself.

The angel Gabriel visited Mary, calling her highly favored. She felt ordinary, but God knew she was more. Most people feel ordinary, but when the Holy Spirit comes on us, the glory of God manifests in our lives and we become extraordinary for God's purpose. Angels are on assignment, waiting to minister to you for God's glory like Gabriel did with Mary.

Did you know that, when you pray, angels stand beside you? When you cry out to God and present your request to Him, an angel is with you. You may say, "Well, I don't see the angel." You can't see your angel with your natural eye, unless they appear as God directs. Many times, you're entertaining angels unaware (Hebrews 13:2). Most of the time, though, you can see angels with your spiritual eyes. When I see an angel moving, I can feel God's presence. When I feel a touch on my right shoulder, I know God is moving in the midst of His people.

When you have an angelic visitation, an angel is coming to bring a message to you or to war against a principality. Even over the body of Moses, the angel of God was fighting a satanic angel, or even Lucifer himself (Jude 9; Deuteronomy 34:5-6). The important point is that, when there is an open heaven, angels come to your rescue. When you make your petition or request, praying through an issue until you feel released, God assigns an angel or angels to you because they're ministering spirits. They're ready to take your words to God.

Another example of angelic presence can be seen when Daniel fasted and prayed for twenty-one days. During that time, he tapped into an open heaven, positioning himself for an encounter. His visitation was available to him, but a principality was trying to block it. Finally, the archangel came to Daniel, telling him that he'd heard Daniel's prayers from the beginning but a principality had stood in his way. Daniel had persisted, though, and after twenty-one days of spiritual warfare, the angel came and ministered strength to him and revealed his purpose.

When you're under an open heaven, angels come to you and they reveal the heart of God. Throughout the entire Bible, you can find angels of God coming to the rescue people in accordance with God's direction. Sarai/Sarah had three angelic visitations, and angels also visited Abraham, telling him that they would have many children even though they were very old.

When you present yourself as a vessel for God to flow through, He will use you. Present yourself as a sacrifice; make yourself available before God. God doesn't ask for much—He just wants you to be available. Are you available for the Master's use? Because God is ready to visit you. These angelic visitations are not only for people in the Bible. God is ready for you to have an encounter with the angelic realm too. He's ready for you to experience a download from heaven until you can say with confidence, "All right. This is what God wants me to do." Prepare to be in awe of your encounters. Don't try to figure it out these experiences with your natural mind—your finite mind is limited. Pray that God would anoint your spiritual eyes and ears so you can see and hear the angels at work.

The Emotional, Human Side of Life

Often, when we are preparing for a visitation, praying deeply and effectively, painful moments from our past will resurface. God cares about our heart and emotions. Psalm 65:9 (NLT) says of God: *"You take care of the earth and water it, making it rich and fertile. The river of God has plenty of water; it provides a bountiful harvest of grain, for you have ordered it so."* When the Holy Spirit brings things back to your mind, it is because He wants to bring healing into those areas of your life.

The Holy Spirit is so sensitive and gentle. He doesn't want you to miss your visitation, so He reveals past hurts so you can deal with them, with His guidance, and bring healing. It may be a level of unforgiveness for another person, or maybe you did something wrong. Whatever the case may be, the Holy Spirit will allow us to see our hearts as though He's holding up a mirror in front of our eyes. When He does that, He's telling us, "I want to heal you in this area so you can have your visitation and not miss God's timing in pouring out the realm of glory." The ministering angels will come to your side as He directs them to aid you in healing.

Sometimes in our walk of faith, as we serve God and honor heaven, we can lose sight of caring for the human aspects of our beings: our emotions and our physical bodies. Elijah saw the glory of God, he saw the fire come down from Heaven. He had amazing encounters with God, but not long after those powerful moments, he fell into a deep depression. The Bible tells us in First Kings 19:4:

> *Then he went on alone into the wilderness, traveling all day. He sat down under a solitary broom tree and*

prayed that he might die. "I have had enough, Lord,"
he said. "Take my life, for I am no better than my
ancestors who have already died."

Then God in His ever-faithful grace and mercy sent an angel
to Elijah:

> *Then **the angel of the Lord came again and***
> ***touched him** and said, "Get up and eat some more,*
> *or the journey ahead will be too much for you." So*
> *he got up and ate and drank, and the food gave him*
> *enough strength to travel forty days and forty nights*
> *to Mount Sinai, the mountain of God. There he came*
> *to a cave, where he spent the night* (1 Kings 19:7-9
> NLT).

Here is the mighty prophet of God hiding in a cave. He had
seen God's glory. He saw fire come down from heaven and destroy
false prophets. But he got depressed, despondent, and he felt ready
to quit. He was having a bit of a pity party: "Oh, it's just me now.
I'm all alone, the only one left." Elijah felt spiritually burnt-out,
oppressed, and discouraged.

> *But the Lord said to him, "What are you doing here,*
> *Elijah?" Elijah replied, "I have zealously served the*
> *Lord God Almighty. But the people of Israel have*
> *broken their covenant with you, torn down your*
> *altars, and killed every one of your prophets. I am the*
> *only one left, and now they are trying to kill me, too"*
> (1 Kings 19:9-10 NLT).

When you come down from those glory-filled mountaintop experiences with God and return to the human side of life, it's important to watch over your emotions. During times of visitation experiences, emotions may want to take over. But don't allow your human emotions to invade your spiritual encounters. Even though you just saw the glory, the flesh of your humanity can shade the experience. Like Elijah, you may feel like the strength of God is no longer there. It doesn't matter how great your anointing, everyone falls prey to the enemy one time or another. Believers can fall prey to discouragement and/or oppression. The important thing is getting back up and getting back into His plan for your life. You have to rise up, take life your life back by force because the violent take it by force (Matthew 11:12). You have to get violent in your faith. Be aggressive, and you'll see what God can do.

There are always areas of your life that God has to fine-tune. We are all being shaped on the Potter's wheel, and we need to stay there until everything ungodly in your life has been taken out. Pray every day for God to increase in you, that He will mold you and make you into His likeness. Ask Him to take out every trace of what He doesn't like and put in what He wants you to have. Ask Him to show you the areas that you have yet to yield to Him. Ask Him how His glory can affect your life. If you pray that daily, you will hear from Him. I promise you that.

When Stephen was being stoned, he looked up toward Heaven. He didn't look around at who was stoning him. He looked up and saw Jesus standing at the right hand of the heavenly Father. What an honor it is to know that, when you give your life to the Lord,

He stands up and recognizes your sacrifice. Everything you go through is for a purpose.

God is with you every step of the way—on the mountaintops and in the caves:

> Then He said, "Go out, and stand on the mountain before the Lord." And behold, the Lord passed by, and a great and strong wind tore into the mountains and broke the rocks in pieces before the Lord, but the Lord was not in the wind; and after the wind an earthquake, but the Lord was not in the earthquake; and after the earthquake a fire, but the Lord was not in the fire; and after the fire a still small voice.

God was with Elijah every moment, and He revealed Himself in a still small voice. You have to learn how to trust the Lord even when you can't see Him or feel Him. No matter what, you can choose to praise Him. Dance when you don't feel like dancing. Give Him a shout even when you feel like you've lost your voice. Why? Because when you do, you attract the angels toward you, and His glory will begin to manifest. You don't move by feeling. You move by faith. When you can't see or feel Him, keep trusting Him.

TRUST GOD

Learning how to trust God even when you can't see or feel Him is crucial for your physical, mental, relational, and—especially— your spiritual life. We may think we are "all in," trusting Him with our whole being, but so did Peter. And then he denied Christ three times. And let's not forget John the Baptist:

> *And John, calling two of his disciples to him, sent*
> *them to Jesus, saying, "Are You the Coming One, or*
> *do we look for another?" When the men had come to*
> *Him [Jesus], they said, "John the Baptist has sent us*
> *to You, saying, 'Are You the Coming One, or do we*
> *look for another?'" (Luke 7:19-20).*

John the Baptist actually baptized Jesus. He saw the heavens open and the Holy Spirit descend like a dove onto Jesus. But persecution had begun and John was incarcerated for preaching the Gospel. He was locked up and began to second-guess himself, maybe thinking, *I wonder if that's the right guy I baptized. Is He really the Christ? Is He really the fulfillment of prophecy? Is He really the One?*

What changes when we go from glory back to the human side of us? What is it about our human nature that causes us to doubt God? If John the Baptist doubted, you and I most likely will doubt one time or another. He heard the heavenly Father telling Jesus He was proud of Him; but not long after, he was questioning if Jesus really was the Messiah.

So, while Jesus was performing miracles, John sent two men to ask Him if He is really the "Coming One." In essence he's saying, "I'm locked up. I'm about to be beheaded. I need to know if You're really the One. I don't want to lose my head for nothing. I need to know." The passage in Luke 7 continues:

> *And that very hour He [Jesus] cured many of infir-*
> *mities, afflictions, and evil spirits; and to many blind*
> *He gave sight. Jesus answered and said to them, "Go*

and tell John the things you have seen and heard: that the blind see, the lame walk, the lepers are cleansed, the deaf hear, the dead are raised, the poor have the gospel preached to them. And blessed is he who is not offended because of Me" (Luke 7:21-23).

Your human side is vulnerable to the attacks of the enemy. You must wear the whole armor of God to deflect attacks (see Ephesians 6:10-18). When you are fighting the battles of the mind, the armor of God will protect you; when you resist the devil, he will flee. Stand on the Word of God. Doubt can creep in anytime. You have to be aware of both the spirit of doubt and the spirit of fear, but also how the spirit of faith can overcome both. You have to trust Him even when you can't trace Him.

Isaiah 59:19 tells us: *"So shall they fear the name of the Lord from the west, and His glory from the rising of the sun; when the enemy comes in like a flood, the Spirit of the Lord will lift up a standard against him."*

When the devil comes in like a flood, the Holy Spirit will overflow you with joy. He will drown your enemies! Remember the armies of Egypt when they were snapping at the heels of Moses and the army of Israel? God drowned them all, because no weapon formed against God's children will prevail! (See Isaiah 54:17.) You and I shall stand—if we learn how to guard our emotions.

We must remember that, *"You [God] will keep in perfect peace all who trust in you, all whose thoughts are fixed on you!"* (Isaiah 26:3 NLT). If you want to experience perfect peace in your mind and spirit, focus on your heavenly Father, Jesus His Son, and the Holy Spirit, your Comforter and Helper. He will hold you in the palms of His hands during every raging storm. When the winds are howling and the waves are crashing, you can stand firm and know that you are a God-purposed person.

You're not going to be defeated. You're not going under—you're going *over*. Keep a positive attitude and take every opportunity to worship in the midst of the battle. David wrote:

> **Lift up your heads**, O you gates! And be lifted up, you everlasting doors! And the King of glory shall come in. **Who is this King of glory? The Lord strong and mighty, the Lord mighty in battle. Lift up your heads**, O you gates! Lift up, you everlasting doors! And the King of glory shall come in. Who is this King of glory? The Lord of hosts, **He is the King of glory** (Psalm 24:7-10).

Discouragement is the spirit of oppression. There is a difference between demonic oppression and demonic possession. When a person is demonically possessed, there is a demonic spirit in them. When someone is oppressed, a demonic spirit is attached to you. But you can break the spirit of oppression. The spirit of heaviness breaks when you put on the garment of praise—when you wear praise and worship as your clothing, as part of who you are in Christ.

You may ask, "How do I do that, preacher?"

Praise God with songs and rejoicing.

"I don't really feel like praising God."

Well, there are some mornings when I wake up and I don't *feel* like praising God either, but I press through those feelings because

I know that He is worthy of my praise every minute of every day. I pursue Him and His presence and my feelings follow. When I start praising, all of a sudden, I'm reminded of His goodness. *"I would have lost heart, unless I had believed that I would see the goodness of the Lord In the land of the living"* (Psalm 27:13).

Jesus told the men to tell John that they saw blind eyes opened, lepers cleansed, the dead raised to life—they saw signs, wonders, and miracles. When you see those kinds of miracles, doubt and disbelief will be cast out.

Don't let the devil abort your destiny because you're temporarily discouraged. Shake yourself off, and remember that it's just a test. Tell yourself, "I'm going to pass this test. I'm going to be promoted, because God's intention is that I carry His glory with me to serve Him others." Look to Heaven, and you will see Jesus standing at the right hand of the Father, looking down at you. Hear Him say, "My child, I'm pleased with you. I'm pleased with your sacrifice. I saw your tears. I have heard your requests. I've seen your heart. I know what you are going through—and now, your rewards are going to be great."

Don't allow the devil to place doubt into your mind. Don't listen when he says you've sacrificed a lot and it might not mean a thing. Or that you gave up everything and you won't receive anything in return. Don't give the devil any room in your mind or your spirit!

Listen, God's going to reward you far greater than what you gave up in order to accomplish His purpose. He'll do exceedingly, abundantly, above all you ever ask or think. You just need to lift your hands up and praise Him. Thank God that He loves you, He calls you, and wants to use you. You may not feel Him at times. You may not even hear Him at times. But get up and praise Him anyway. Get up and shake yourself happy. When you do, you'll find the spirit of heaviness has been broken. Praise Him, and realize that after weeping comes joy!

THE VALLEY OF WEEPING

We all have and will experience times of weeping. There are usually two causes for weeping: 1) times of testing or trials that bring weeping; and 2) times of joyful weeping, which can be an expression of gratitude toward God. These can be moments when you're so thankful for the presence of God that tears stream from your eyes. You're so thankful that tears stream from your eyes because you appreciate the presence of God. We must remember that God will supply all of our needs according to His riches, not according to how we're feeling (see Philippians 4:19). Even when we are faced with the valley of weeping in our own lives, and in the lives of others, we know that God is with us.

Often, God will put detours in our path when we follow Him. When Peter and John were going to the temple to pray, they encountered a beggar asking for money:

> *And fixing his eyes on him, with John, Peter said, "Look at us." So he gave them his attention, expecting to receive something from them. Then Peter said,* **"Silver and gold I do not have, but what I do have I give you: In the name of Jesus Christ of Nazareth, rise up and walk."** *And he took him by*

*the right hand and lifted him up, and immediately his feet and ankle bones received strength. **So he, leaping up, stood and walked** and entered the temple with them—walking, leaping, and **praising God**. And all the people saw him walking and praising God. Then they knew that it was he who sat begging alms at the Beautiful Gate of the temple; and they were filled with wonder and amazement at what had happened to him* (Acts 3:4-10).

Like Peter and John, you may not have silver or gold to give, but you *do* have something you can offer someone, to your family, your community, and to the world. No matter what the problem, you have the answer in you because of the Holy Spirit and the access you have to spiritual gifts. Don't keep the answer to yourself. You have the remedy for what ails people. If you know someone is struggling with an illness, you can pray for that person, or you can let the problem overwhelm you until you say, "Well, I can't do this." Yes, you can. Pray. Just step out into the spiritual realm and pray. Your prayer is exactly what the person needs. Just say, "In the name of Jesus, I command this cancer to die, or this headache to go away, or these blind eyes to see, whatever the case may be."

Reaching out to people is the way of the Lord Jesus Christ. He reached out to the suffering with His compassion and with miraculous healing. When people are in the valley of weeping, they often don't want to face inner conflicts and outward struggles. They don't have the energy to identify with what is really going on inside of them. They may even want to keep it a secret.

But when they seek counsel and God's wisdom, they will come to a place of freedom. Through the gifts of the Spirit, as believers, we can help others with their heavy burdens. We can shine a light on God's goodness and mercy during their time of devastation or tragedy, helping to turn their weeping into rejoicing.

I want to encourage you with a little bit of my personal testimony, and I pray it will build your faith. I share this with you not for sympathy but for you to understand that God is a miracle-working God. You can overcome the tragedies of life—you really can. The place of sorrowful weeping is not eternal. It's just a moment in time.

I've been in the miracle and healing ministry for a long time. I have traveled up and down the East Coast, West Coast, and all across the United States. I've traveled through developing countries, and I've seen many miracles including the dead raised, blind eyes opened, people walking up out of their wheelchairs, and even a finger grows out. I've seen God do incredible miracles.

After I returned home from a healing revival one day, I hugged my young daughter and carried her into her room. I took out my guitar, singing her a song that I always used to sing during Oral Robert's crusades, "When My Savior Reached Down His Hands for Me." She always liked it when I sang to her, and she smiled back at me as I was singing. Then, I laid her down in her crib for a nap.

Later that day, my wife and I noticed something was wrong with our daughter.

And, by nighttime, she still wasn't acting right, so we took her to the hospital. By 2 A.M. the next morning, she had slipped into the hands of God.

About six months before that, I'd had a dream and our daughter said to me, "Daddy, I'm getting ready to leave you." I woke up with tears in my eyes. No father wants to even think about losing their child. So, I ran to her and held her closely. I said, "What are you trying to tell me, baby girl? What are you trying to say to me?" She said, "Daddy, I'm leaving you. Your hardest test is ahead of you, but the angel is going to walk with you."

My wife and I were at the hospital when she passed and, as I was holding her for the last time, I cried out to God: "Lord, how am I going to be able to bear this? I've been here for others. I've preached thousands of messages. I lay hands on hundreds of people and have seen every kind of miracle documented by doctors. Why is my daughter going to die, God?" It doesn't hurt to question God. God is not offended if you question Him when you go through trials. I've heard some people say not to question God, but get that out your mind. That's nonsense. You're human. He wants you to express how you're hurting. That's how He heals you through the Holy Spirit.

Two months after her death, I felt so discouraged that I told Jack Cole Jr., "I'm done with the healing miracle ministry." Well, Jack called Robert Schambach and he said that he wanted to see me, "immediately." Jack Cole Jr. had told Robert what I was going through. When I met with Schambach, he laid his hands on me and said, "You're going to carry the glory of God. You're going to see what I did not see." I don't remember the prophecy word for word, but when he laid his hands on my shoulder he said, "You're going to see miracles as never before. God knows something you don't know." I went home, still in deep, inner pain. But, then an angel and the Holy Spirit began to visit me.

I spent time just healing from my grief. I knew I wouldn't be good to anyone if God didn't heal me. After some time, healing began to manifest in my life. On one of our ordinary Wednesday night Bible study, I taught like I normally do. A grandmother came in the room with a little girl. The little girl's lungs were undeveloped, so she was on oxygen. She also had autism and three holes in her heart.

After the service, I prayed for everybody else, but I thought to myself, *I'm not going to pray for that child. I'm not going to lay my hands on her, because I know God's going to heal that child. And that's going to make me mean and madder than fire.* I'm just being honest with you. If God healed that girl, He was going to make me angry. I thought, *I'm not going to do it. I will lay hands on everybody else.*

The child was lying in a little basket, and I could see tears in the grandmother's eyes. All of a sudden, I looked to my right, and—as God is my witness—my little girl showed up, pulled at my pant leg, and said to me, "Daddy, that's not right. Let's go down there and lay hands on that little girl." I was in tears, because I knew God was going to give her a miracle. So, I went over and laid my hands on that baby; 24 hours later, she had a doctor appointment. God had given that little girl two new lungs—no more oxygen tank. She was healed from autism and had no holes in her heart.

I said, "God, I don't understand You."

Robert Schambach, Jack Cole, and my other mentors taught me, "God always knows something you don't." So, if you are in a valley of weeping, if you have faced a tragedy, don't stop believing and don't stop fulfilling your God-given assignment. I've got good news for you. *The devil's not fighting you for where you are, but where you're going.* You must keep pursuing the heart of God. It's time for His visitation.

Let me pray for you.

> *Father, in the name of Jesus, I pray that You would bless this reader, encourage and lift up this person to be all You want and need for Your Kingdom glory. You are the God of more than enough. You are the God of miracles. There's no distance between You and this friend of Yours, because prayers reach You directly. I pray this reader would get up and shake off anything that's holding them back from freedom and joy. Amen.*

God bless you.

PRAYER OF IMPARTATION

> *Father, in the name of Jesus, we thank you for this Kairos moment, this time of visitation that you are revealing to each individual. Show them how important the role of the Holy Spirit and His gifts are in their lives. Let them receive this time of visitation and the impartation of His gifts as never before in their lives. In Jesus' name, amen.*

> *And when the Lord saw that he turned aside to see, God called unto him out of the midst of the bush,*

and said, Moses, Moses. And he said, Here am I
(Exodus 3:4 KJV).

9 | GOD'S EVERY WORD

But Jesus told him, "No! The Scriptures say,
'People do not live by bread alone, but by every
word that comes from the mouth of God.'"
—Matthew 4:4 NLT

*I*n this final chapter, we are going to discuss the intrinsic value of every word that comes from the mouth of God—and how it affects the glory of God in your life. The very beginning of the Bible says, *"In the beginning...God said..."* (Genesis 1:1-3). And then, again, John's Gospel begins, *"In the beginning was the Word, and the Word was with God, and the Word was God"* (John 1:1). God speaks, and He has no shortage of words. Every time you seek Him, every time you call on Him, He will answer and give you a word. God will never stop talking to you. The more you pursue Him, the more He talks to you.

Deuteronomy 8:3 says:

> *So He humbled you, allowed you to hunger, and fed you with manna which you did not know nor did your fathers know, that He might make you know that* **man shall not live by bread alone; but man lives by every word that proceeds from the mouth of the Lord.**

God's Word is so very valuable that its importance is cited throughout the Bible. When you move in obedience to His word, walking the steps of faith and serving others, you unlock the glory of God and tap into His heart.

The life of Abraham reveals the power of God's Word to build His kingdom on the earth. In Genesis 22, we can see a faith-filled man clinging to the word of God above all else, even above the love he had for his only son.

> *Now it came to pass after these things that* **God tested Abraham, and said to him,** *"Abraham!" And he said, "Here I am." Then He said, "Take now your son, your only son Isaac, whom you love, and go to the land of Moriah, and offer him there as a burnt offering on one of the mountains of which I shall tell you." So Abraham rose early in the morning and saddled his donkey, and took two of his young men with him, and Isaac his son; and he split the wood for the burnt offering, and arose and went to the place*

of which God had told him. Then on the third day Abraham lifted his eyes and saw the place afar off. And Abraham said to his young men, "Stay here with the donkey; the lad and I will go yonder and worship, and we will come back to you."

*So Abraham took the wood of the burnt offering and laid it on Isaac his son; and he took the fire in his hand, and a knife, and the two of them went together. But Isaac spoke to Abraham his father and said, "My father!" And he said, "Here I am, my son." Then he said, "Look, the fire and the wood, but where is the lamb for a burnt offering?" And Abraham said, "My son, **God will provide** for Himself the lamb for a burnt offering." So the two of them went together* (Genesis 22:1-8).

Isaac understood the importance of sacrifice, because he'd been taught to follow God by his father. But this time the obedience of Abraham was being tested. How far would he go to see the hand of God demonstrate power in his life and reveal the glory? God wanted to reveal Abraham's heart through this test, so that He could lead him into the next assignment of his life—a father to nations.

But, first, Abraham would have to surrender everything. At the beginning of the Genesis 22 passage, God gave Abraham direction. His word directed Abraham *"to go to the land of Moriah...to one of the mountains."* So, Abraham and Isaac went to Moriah without knowing what the plan was, or even exactly which mountain God wanted them to climb. I tell people all the time, especially young preachers, God will give you steps A, B, and C, and then He'll give you step G. He won't reveal D, E, F—those you'll have to figure out for yourself. At times, you might be thinking, *Oh Lord God, what is the next step in Your plan? What's going to happen next?* In the midst of that wondering, though, you have to remember that He is the Alpha and Omega—the beginning and the end. He's the entire alphabet, so He knows every step. With this in mind, you can declare your absolute trust and dependence on Him.

Abraham's journey depicts an important step we have to take in our walk of faith. Sometimes, when God gives you a promise, He wants to see if the promise is going to overtake you. Are you more dedicated to the promise than the Promiser? Abraham waited for years for his son who had been promised to him by the Lord. But God wanted to know if His word was more valuable to Abraham than anything else. As Abraham followed God's direction, he showed his dedication with every step. How many times has God asked you to do something, but you said, "Lord, it's unbearable, I can't do it." How many times has He challenged your faith? How many times has He challenged your obedience? He's asking you today to walk in obedience and then see how your faith will come alive.

So, Abraham rose up early in the morning, following God's Word, and left with his son. We're not told if Abraham mentioned his trip to Sarah. I imagine he didn't tell her, though. I don't think any husband in their right mind would tell their wife that he was going to kill their long-awaited promised child. Sarah would probably have called him crazy, never allowing him to take Isaac. So,

I imagine Abraham kept this mission to himself. I think it was something between him, Isaac, and the angel of the Lord. There are certain things God requires from you that He wouldn't require from another individual. This wasn't Sarah's test; it was Abraham's.

On the third day of their journey, Abraham lifted his eyes and saw the place he was supposed to go. At this point, Abraham told the young servants to stay behind. He realized that the obedience and dedication he was being asked for by the Lord was not required of anyone else. Abraham would have been taking on a false responsibility to try to force his level of faith on anyone else. This is a mistake many people make. When you've encountered God, living in obedience to Him, all you can do is be a teaching voice to others. You can't force people to follow Christ; you can't make people surrender to God's plan or pursue the gifts of the Spirit through the Holy Spirit baptism. Abraham knew that he could make his servant's go with him up the mountain, but that they would have to be called by the Lord for themselves, so he wisely left them behind.

> Then they came to the place of which **God had told him**. And Abraham built an altar there and placed the wood in order; and he bound Isaac his son and laid him on the altar, upon the wood. And Abraham stretched out his hand and took the knife to slay his son. But the Angel of the Lord called to him from heaven and said, "Abraham, Abraham!" So he said, "Here I am." And He said, "Do not lay your hand on the lad, or do anything to him; for now I know that

you fear God, since you have not withheld your son,
your only son, from Me" (Genesis 22:9-12).

Many times, tests from the Lord feel overwhelming and terrifying. You may wonder, *Lord, how can I pass this test?* Let Abraham be your example in this. With each test, keep your focus on your heavenly Father, listen for His voice alone, and keep your attitude aligned with the goodness of God. When you keep your focus on what God is saying, your spirit locked onto Him, He will keep you in perfect peace. Because of Abraham's obedience and total devotion to God, the heavens were opened for him. He stepped out in faith, surrendering his most precious son, and God unlocked the glory over him. God's blessing and promise would surround Abraham's life, because he valued the word of God above all else.

Then Abraham lifted his eyes and looked, and there
behind him was a ram caught in a thicket by its horns.
So Abraham went and took the ram, and offered it up
for a burnt offering instead of his son. And Abraham
called the name of the place, The-Lord-Will-Provide;
as it is said to this day, "In the Mount of the Lord it
shall be provided." Then the Angel of the Lord called
to Abraham a second time out of heaven, and said:
"By Myself I have sworn, **says the Lord,** *because you*
have done this thing, and have not withheld your son,
your only son— **blessing I will bless you, and mul-**
tiplying I will multiply your descendants *as the*
stars of the heaven and as the sand which is on the
seashore; and your descendants shall possess the gate
of their enemies. In your seed all the nations of the

*earth shall be blessed, **because you have obeyed My voice***" (Genesis 22:13-18).

These mountaintop experiences—Abraham with Isaac or Moses before the burning bush—come from treasuring every word that proceeds from the mouth of God. With this test, God taught Abraham about the value of persistent faith. Facing a challenge fully dependent on God will allow a champion to burst out from inside of you. God knew that there was a champion within Abraham, and He is bringing forth a champion in you as well.

By testing Abraham, God wasn't setting him up to sin, but rather to grow. God will never test you to walk away from Him. He wants you to follow Him in righteousness, line by line, precept by precept. He wants you to be obedient. He wants you to be used by Him. He will convict your heart when you're wrong, but God will never lead you away from His presence. He encourages you to continue following His pathway laid before you.

> **The Lord directs the steps** of the godly. He delights
> in **every detail** of their lives (Psalm 37:23 NLT).

The steps of a good person are ordered of the Lord. Because your steps are ordered by God, you must continue trusting Him and following in obedience. There is no trial that you face that could surprise God. He has placed victory and abundant life are right around the corner.

Abraham passed his test with flying colors. Each of us will go through many tests in our lives, and, like Abraham, we have to determine to pass each one. Ask yourself, *What would be the consequence of disobedience?* It's better to be willing and obedient than suffer the consequences of being disobedient. And, on the other side of obedience, is God's blessing. It's strange how God works sometimes. The very thing you're holding onto, you often must release. But, when God's involved, nothing leaves your hand without it returning bigger and better.

God offered up His only Son for the redemption of all humankind. Jesus died on the Cross so that you and I could live on earth for His glory and live eternally with Him. We can be victorious when tested in life because He gives us spiritual gifts that are more powerful than what the world can set before us. So, don't give up when the assignment seems too much to bear. After a spiritual attack is over and the curse is broken, it's breakthrough time.

Don't throw in the towel. There's a miracle that's about to manifest for you. All you have to do is continue in obedience. God will continue to talk you through whatever troubles come your way. Every word that comes from His mouth is either direction, encouragement, or a battle plan strategy for what you need. He will guide you. From the mouth of God to you, for His glory.

What are you willing to walk away from so you can get that breakthrough? Whatever you're willing to surrender will bring you into a place where you receive your miracle. What are you willing to walk away from so you can see the tangible evidence of the miraculous hands of God? There's tangible evidence that God is ready to manifest.

PROPHETIC DECLARATION

The Holy Spirit is with you right now. He's ready to touch you with the anointing oil from on high. Father, I release the anointing of angels into this reader's life—into the person's home and family. I pray, now, that the angels of God—His ministering spirits—will carry out every assignment that touches this reader's life.

I pray that the angel of God would take every prayer request, bring it before the throne of God, and present it as a sacrifice, a seed of obedience. I ask that the angel of God would go now and release the healing power of God. I come against sin, sickness, and every form of disease in the name of Jesus. I curse cancer. I curse diabetes. I curse AIDS. I command glaucoma to be healed. I command blind eyes to be opened, deaf ears to hear. I command all this in the mighty name of Jesus.

God is touching you and giving you a miracle. There's a breakthrough anointing on your life. The anointing doesn't just break sin and sickness, it destroys it. You don't have to know me personally, just receive the words of knowledge; receive the prayer by the unction of the Holy Spirit.

If you are not baptized in the Holy Spirit, I want to pray that you get baptized. You need to go to the next level. Thank God you attend a good church. Thank God you are saved. That's the greatest miracle of all. Now you need to be sanctified, separated, sold out for the Lord. Give your very best to Him. Maybe you never spoke in tongues or received your prayer language.

Father, this gift is imparted to my reader, Your child. I pray for this person to receive the baptism of the Holy Spirit and speak in tongues as You reveal what gift You want to operate through in their lives.

If you're in ministry and you feel like you want to quit ministry, please pray about your decision. God needs you to share the

Gospel with the world. Whether you're an apostle, prophet, evangelist, pastor, or teacher, I want to encourage you as a prophet of God that He has seen your dedication and your sacrifice. Your ministry is getting ready to take a turn. Get ready for a paradigm shift. Something good is about to take place for you.

Pastor, don't be discouraged; an influx of people are coming into your ministry. You have been faithful, just like David, over the few sheep. But you have been prophesied to be a king. Well, God's setting the stage for you to get the king's crown, walk in victory, and be a giant killer. Open the regions, speak into the regions, open the geographical areas that have been held back and break that demonic powers.

I speak to the far reaches of your ministry that's been holding back your finances and your miracle. I command that demonic spirits, the strong man over the city, be broken. I command deliverance to take place. Agree with me that demonic power is going to be destroyed in the mighty name of Jesus Christ of Nazareth.

If you don't have peace, if you have inner conflict, a spirit of unforgiveness, you're harboring bitterness, or have been rejected, I want to pray for you. God, heal this person's spirit and inward conflicts. Reveal Your love, grace, and mercy to this reader, Lord. Take away the agony, the hurt, and the pain. Reveal that You are getting ready to anoint this reader with great influence.

You're going to use God's positive influence to touch many people, many lives.

Your God is the God of signs, wonders, and miracles. Reach out right now with your hands lifted toward Heaven. See the nail-scarred hands of Jesus reaching down from Heaven's balcony to embrace you. He will pull you out of that valley of weeping and place you on the mountaintop of rejoicing.

God is for you, so there is no adversary, enemy, or situation in life than can overtake you. You will fulfill the purpose of God. You are a purposeful person; you're future possessed.

Yesterday's tomb is tomorrow's womb. In other words, you're coming out of a place of death to a place of life. You're coming out of a place of weeping to a place of joy. After sorrow comes great joy. I release joy on you to cover the places of sorrow.

I release happiness, double for your trouble. God's taking all the chaos and He's giving you peace that surpasses all understanding. This is a time for miracles—nothing's impossible with God.

All you have to do is just *believe* God's Word, *stand* on His Word. And, as I pray for you right now, you need to know that He's the God of more than enough. Something good is about to happen to you. I've learned this to be the truth—many times your miracle comes through the aid of helping someone else. So, I pray that God will use you to touch someone else's life for His glory.

> *Father, I pray that this reader will rise to the occasion and be a blessing to others. Whether just a smile for someone who's going through a time of sorrow, darkness, or grief, or a prayer for a neighbor, or a hospital visit—whatever God lays on your heart to do, I pray you obey.*
>
> *I pray that You, Lord, would speak into this friend's life. Let the nine gifts of the Holy Spirit begin to operate right now. Let the baptism of the Holy Spirit begin to manifest. Let the anointing and the greater*

glory shine on this person, God, because I see glory coming right now. Friend, just reach your hands up by the act of faith and move on faith. Lift your hands up and say, "I receive the greater glory. I'm going to walk in the supernatural. I am what God says I am. I'm going to do what God says I can do. I'm going to be what God says I can be. And I'm not going to allow my past to dictate my future. I'm not what the world says I am. I'm not what the devil says I am. I am what God says I am. I'm going to fulfill the great commission and the calling on my life." Amen.

I'm praying right now in agreement with you. As Jesus tells us, *"Again I say to you that if two of you agree on earth concerning anything that they ask, it will be done for them by My Father in heaven. For where two or three are gathered together in My name, I am there in the midst of them"* (Matthew 18:19-20). As we two shall touch and agree it will be done for us according to God's will.

I speak blessings over your life. I speak miracles over you, and I believe that the greatest is about to take place in your life. Your greatest days are ahead of you. Don't give up. Your darkest days are behind you and your greatest days are ahead.

It's time for the heavenly keys to unlock the supernatural in your life and for you to access your spiritual gifts. It's time to carry a supernatural anointing into the world around you. It's time for God to stand up like He did in Stephen's defense, recognizing your good works in obedience to Him.

I encourage you keep on keeping on. Don't stop—there's a miracle with your name on it.

God bless you.

PRAYER OF IMPARTATION

Father, in Jesus' name, we thank You for every preceding word that comes from the mouth of God. I pray that today that every word God speaks, that everyone will come to an understand that man shall not live by bread alone, but by every Word that proceedeth out of the mouth of God. I pray that they take that word, obey it, and walk out God's plan and be empowered by the Holy Spirit and allow the Holy Spirit to use them to fulfill their great commission. In Jesus' name, amen.

But he answered and said, It is written, Man shall not live by bread alone, but by every word that proceedeth out of the mouth of God (Matthew 4:4 KJV).

ABOUT THE AUTHOR

Known as America's Sackcloth Prophet, Tracy Cooke established Cooke Revivals Ministry to bring God's revival message through miracles, signs, and wonders.

Tracy Cooke received the gift of salvation and gave not only his heart but also his life to God in November 1992. In December 1993, he answered the call to preach the gospel of Jesus Christ. In his earlier years, he served as an assistant pastor of a local assembly where he served diligently in covering the ministry in prayer, teaching Bible School, and assisting the pastor in discipling the saints.

Tracy has spent many years traveling as an evangelist throughout America and the world bringing the truth of God's Word back to the heart of His people. He has ministered on radio and television and is not only known for the power of the prophetic anointing that rests upon his ministry, but also for the ministry of signs, wonders, and miracles.

He is the founder of Elisha Training Center, the school of the prophets, where he trains and mentors the next generation in the prophetic gifting and calling for the next move of God.

Thousands have been healed and blessed through the calling on Tracy's life. He has been a frequent guest on Sid Roth's *It's Supernatural!* as well as a recurring guest speaker on platforms spanning the world such as King Jesus Ministries with Guillermo Maldonado.

Tracy currently lives in New Bern, NC, with his wife and ministry partner, Shawn.